D1084614

THE ORVIS POCKET GUIDE TO FLY FISHING FOR

Bonefish and Permit

Books by Jack Samson

Line Down!: The Special World of Big Game Fishing
The Best of Corey Ford
The Sportsman's World
The Worlds of Ernest Thompson Seton
Falconry Today
Successful Outdoor Writing
The Bear Book
The Pond
The Grizzly Book
The Great Fish
Modern Falconry
Hunting The Southwest
Chennault: A Biography
Salt Water Fly Fishing
Billfish on a Fly
Lee Wulff: A Biography
Permit on a Fly
Wind Knots & Near Misses

The Orvis Pocket Guide to Fly Fishing for
Bonefish and Permit

Jack Samson

The Lyons Press

To Victoria

Printed in China

10 9 8 7 6 5 4 3 2 1

Library of Congress Cataloging-in-Publication Data

Samson, Jack.
    The Orvis pocket guide to fly fishing for bonefish and permit /
    Jack Samson.
        p. cm.
    ISBN 1-58574-075-6
        1. Bonefishing. 2. Permit fishing. 3. Saltwater fly fishing.
I. Title: Fly fishing for bonefish and permit. II. Title.

    SH691.B6 S26 2001
    799.1′743—dc21

                                                        00-48155

CONTENTS

ACKNOWLEDGMENTS

I cannot thank enough those saltwater fly-fishing friends and guides—Al McClane, Billy Pate, Dick Williams, Billy Knowles, George Hommell, Nelson Bryant, Hal Chittum, Bill Curtis, Will Bauer, Gil Drake Jr., Hank Brown, Rick Ruoff, Winston Moore, Robert Hyde, Lincoln Westby, David Westby and the late Joel Westby, Robert "Dubs" Young, Jan Isley, Tom Woodward, Gordie Hill, and a consortium of saltwater flats fly fishermen—who took the time to teach me the flats, the fish that inhabit them, and the techniques used to catch them.

The late Gene Hill

And, indeed, I am indebted to the others—Lefty Kreh, Mark Sosin, Dick Brown, the late Jimmie Albright, Lou Tabory, Cam Sigler, Vic Dunaway, Nick Curcione, Bill Barnes, the late Harry Kime, the late Joe Brooks, Jim Chapralis, the late Frank Woolner, Mike Leech, Didier van der Veecken, Terry Baird, Brendan Banahan, Dick Born, Jack Charlton, Sonja Lillvik, Bobby Settles, Doug Schlink, Pat Pendergast, Bob Nauheim, Joe Fisher, Tommy Gay, Craig Hayes, Ted Juracsik, Harry Tennison, Joe Hudson, and (last, but never least, my friend) the late Gene Hill—for helping me gather material for this book.

JACK SAMSON
Santa Fe, New Mexico, July 2000

FOREWORD

A friend once told me about a bonefish flat near Key Largo that has a nice hard bottom and is easy to wade. You can drive to it. The one time I fished it, I had not even fully left the car seat when I saw three large bonefish tails waving hello. I saw many nice bonefish that day and never hooked one. Although I probably hit this place on an exceptional day, I still have fantasies of booking a cheap motel nearby and fishing this flat for a week, unencumbered by a boat or anyone else's timetable. Something to guide me through this week of bonefishing was what I had in mind when I asked Jack Samson to write a pocket guide to bonefish and permit.

This is a novice's book, with enough on fly selection, flats habitat, and spotting and approaching fish to get anyone started. I see it as the ideal companion for someone who is exploring the world of bonefish and permit for the first time. It would be a great book to read before your first tropical saltwater trip with a guide. Or perhaps you plan on camping along the Yucatan Peninsula, looking for bonefish flats along the way, as one friend of mine did several years ago. Another buddy spends a month in Puerto Rico each winter and has explored some outlying islands, looking for bonefish on his own. Although he is a seasoned charter boat captain on Cape Cod, he is a novice when it comes to bonefish. This little volume would fit in his carry-on bag and I bet would have been worth its weight in Crazy Charlies on his trip last year.

Pocket guides like this are usually packed with advice and pretty short on entertainment value, but Jack has filled this volume with fascinating stuff on bonefish and permit natural history, the pedigree of some of our more famous saltwater fly patterns, and even a little history of legendary tropical lodges. His vast experience writing and editing for *Field & Stream, Fly Rod & Reel,* and *Saltwater Fly Fishing* has given him a fresh and varied perspective. He appreciates everything about bonefish and permit. He's been around, he's seen most of it—the guy even fished with Al McClane!

You'll probably want to read this book a few times before your next fishing trip, but don't forget to take it with you, tucked neatly in your tackle bag. I bet you'll refer to it often: After good days, you'll want to learn a bit more about the lore of bonefishing history, and after the tough days, you'll want to figure out how you could have done better.

—*Tom Rosenbauer*

INTRODUCTION

THE LURE OF SALTWATER FLY FISHING

My own saltwater fishing career spans a lot of years—from those childhood times in the 1930s on Rhode Island's Narragansett Bay with a hand line as a constant companion to today's pursuit of tropical flats fish with a fly rod.

By the late 1970s, I had caught about all the big saltwater game fish I wanted to on heavy, conventional tackle. When I culminated almost 40 years of big-game fishing with a 1,000-pound-plus Pacific black marlin on 80-pound line at Lizard Island in Australia, I decided to revert to saltwater fly fishing.

When I did, I discovered the genuine excitement of stalking and catching bonefish on the flats with a light fly rod. Fighting big bonefish on a 6-weight fly rod and an 8-pound tippet surpassed any thrill I had ever experienced with big-game fish.

I had been fly fishing most of my life in fresh water when I discovered the fun of fly fishing in the salt in the mid-1960s. I was helping the late Willard F. "Al" Rockwell rebuild Cat Cay in the Bahamas after it had been devastated by Hurricane Betsy in 1965. Rockwell and a consortium of other wealthy industrialists had purchased the lovely little island just south of Bimini from the daughter of the late New York advertising executive, Lou Wasey, and intended to rebuild it into the great recreational island it had been before the hurricane. In addition to marvelous big-game fishing in the Gulf Stream just west of the island, Cat Cay had its own several-mile-long bonefish flat to the east and south of the island. Nobody had fished it since island residents had been forced to evacuate in 1965.

I decided to try for bonefish on a fly, but I hadn't the faintest idea how to do it. Fortunately, my office was in New York City—only a few blocks from the legendary Abercrombie & Fitch store on East 45th Street and Madison Avenue. There I sought the advice of veteran fly fisherman and salesman Emil Schmidt. He made up a list of what I would need—after telling me to put away all my well-used split-bamboo fly rods and reels.

I nearly had a heart attack at the price of the tackle he recommended! He suggested I buy a four-piece 8-weight fiberglass fly rod, a Fin-Nor fly reel, several floating fly lines, several dozen leaders in 8- to 10-pound tippet strength, and an assortment of bonefish flies that included such beauties as Bill Curtis's Blue Tail Fly, Chico Fernandez's Bonefish Special, Bonnie Smith's Tailing Bonefish Fly, Jimmie Albright's Frankee-Belle Bonefish Fly, Carl Navarre's Green Weenie, and George Hommell's Blue Evil Eye—a thoroughly professional selection at that time.

Looking back in amusement at those days, I realize how ill prepared I was for bonefishing. I knew nothing about the habits of the fish, the ecology of a bonefish flat, the techniques needed to catch one on a fly, or what to do with one after I hooked it.

Wading the flat at Cat Cay, Bahamas, 1968.

I began by wading the flats of Cat Cay barefoot—a serious mistake. I almost immediately cut my feet on sharp shells and rough coral. A pair of tennis shoes helped but did not ward off the sharp spines of the many black sea urchins that inhabited the flats. It took me almost a week to realize that the almost invisible, flitting, ghostly shapes I kept seeing in the shallow water of the flat were really *bonefish*. I had been casting flies at boxfish, needlefish, all sorts of snappers and small jacks, barracuda, and small sharks. I lost a number of my coveted flies to the teeth of the little snappers until I realized what they were.

I began my quest for bonefish in March, and by mid-April I was an expert on surface glare, wind-ruffled surfaces, overcast days when I could see nothing, badly burned skin, and chapped lips. I didn't know enough to wear polarized sunglasses. It was late April before I learned how to find bonefish on the incoming tide and had figured out their feeding pattern. Even then I cast flies into the middle of schools, short of the schools, and behind the schools—spooking innumerable bonefish with my leader. I frightened fish by wading right up to them, by waving my casting arm when they were close, and by false-casting right over the schools. I wore bright shirts until I realized that bonefish were fleeing the flat at my approach. I lost so many pre-tied leaders I had to learn to tie all new knots—ones that would hold in salt water. I read everything I could find on bonefish, including Stanley Babson's marvelous book *Bonefishing,* published in 1965.

The last day of April 1968 was a day of triumph. I was crouched—on a clear, still morning—close to the small channel that separates North from South Cat Cay. The tide was pouring in from the Gulf Stream to the west and, as I stared into the clear water ahead of me, I saw a school of bonefish making its way up the channel. They were not feeding yet, but were making their way toward the flat behind me. I had on a Phillips Pink Shrimp—a favorite of the legendary Joe Brooks.

As the fish approached, I dropped the fly a good 12 feet ahead of the school and allowed it to sink. I had not yet learned to strip the fly with my left hand, so all I did was give the fly some small jerks with the rod tip.

To my utter amazement, the lead fish swung to its left and took the pink fly as it moved. I was in such shock that I failed to set the hook! It was probably a good thing, as the swimming fish hooked itself and—

Bonefish.

feeling the hook—streaked for the flat behind me. I had enough sense to raise the rod tip, and the battle was on.

The rest of the small school stayed with the hooked fish for part of the fight but finally left for deeper water. I was stumbling across the flat, in knee-deep water, trying to keep up with the churning bonefish. It headed south along the curve of the flat and easily took out 100 yards of line and backing before I had sense enough to run after it.

The fish finally wore itself out fighting the rod and dragging all that line, and I finally managed to work it into very shallow water along the east side of South Cat Cay. I had no net, so I eased it up on the dry sand and fell upon it like a ravenous osprey. What a thrill! A frigate bird overhead tilted away at my shout of triumph.

I carried that battered bonefish back to the boat docks and showed it to every bored construction worker I could find. I would have had it mounted had there been a taxidermist anywhere near Cat Cay. As it was, one of

Author fighting bonefish, Cat Cay, Bahamas, 1968.

the Bahamian cooks asked me if he could have it to eat. I had no way of preserving it anyway, so I gave it to him—reluctantly. It weighed exactly 6 pounds, 4 ounces on the kitchen scales—a figure I shall never forget.

I have been an avid saltwater fly fisherman since that day. I later learned a lot more about bonefish on the flats (and permit and tarpon and snook, among other game fish) and fished over much of the Bahamas and Florida Keys in the ensuing years. I have caught a couple of bonefish on a fly in the 10-pound category, but never much bigger. A 10 pound bonefish on fly rod is a handful! I have been in on the catching of a 14-pound bonefish in the Yucatan—caught by my friend Will Bauer on a small, green crab fly. I don't ever expect to see a bigger one caught on a fly, but that one was enough to satisfy me for a long time to come.

Author's first bonefish, Cat Cay, 1968.

The following year, legendary *Field & Stream* fishing editor A. J. McClane came down to the island after I had sent both him and his wife an invitation to look at the way Cat Cay was shaping up. By that time I was getting pretty good with the fly rod and had cut a swath through the several schools of bonefish that frequented the Cat Cay flats. I had also flown over to Chub Cay and fished the flats there with Lou Dougherty. I had fished with "Bonefish Sam" Ellis up at Bimini and had begun to consider myself somewhat of an expert. Little did I know I was a mere novice and really knew nothing about saltwater fly fishing yet.

A. J. and I caught some nice bonefish in those few days on the flats, but the real highlight of that visit was the last day, when I accidentally caught a small permit with that same Phillips Pink Shrimp fly.

I was casting to a school of bonefish, and the little permit just happened to pick it up. I tried to act as though it were an everyday event—in spite of my hysterical battle with it—but I suspect A. J. knew I had never even seen one before. It only weighed between 4 and 5 pounds, and we released it, but by then I thought catching a permit on a fly was highly overrated.

I was to cast flies at scores of permit in the next few years, but it was *18 years later* before I caught my second permit on a fly, on Turneffe Island in Belize!

For my money, there is no greater thrill than catching bonefish and permit on a fly rod. I expect to be doing it happily until I go to the great bonefish flat in the sky. I have only one regret: I could have saved myself a whole lot of agony, time, and effort in catching my first bonefish on a fly had somebody written a pocket guide like this back in the mid-1960s!

CHAPTER 1

FLATS FISH

BONEFISH

The bonefish *(Albula vulpes)* is a unique, shallow-water game fish, the only living member of its genus. It belongs to a family (Albulidae) of very primitive bony fish that date back to the Cretaceous period—125 million years ago.

Though they can attain a weight of 20 pounds or more, the average weight of bonefish caught in the Bahamas, Florida Keys, and the Caribbean is 4 to 6 pounds. Anything more than 8 pounds is generally considered a big bonefish. Bonefish of 20 pounds or

The bonefish.

more are usually found in deep water off such places as East Africa or Hawaii.

Bonefish tend to spend their time at low tides in the deeper channels and holes and sometimes in the deep water off reefs, moving up onto the shallow flats to eat on the incoming tide and high tides. Bonefish root in the bottom mud of the flats with their snouts, eating a huge variety of creatures, including marine worms, mollusks, crabs, squid, small fish, a whole family of shrimp, and even the spiny sea urchins. Bonefish have specialized granular plates or crushers both on the upper jaw and on top of the tongue, which allow them to grind or crush their prey before swallowing it. Even large mollusks can be broken and ground up by these crushers. Anglers who have stuck a finger in a bonefish's mouth can attest to the strength of these plates!

Bonefish are extremely difficult to see, even in shallow water. Hundreds of small, shiny scales cover a fish's body and reflect sunlight until you could swear it is invisible.

A bonefish has a large, forked tail that can send it across the flats at 25 miles per hour when frightened by any number of predators that inhabit its world—barracuda; sharks; big jacks; man; and such overhead dangers as pelicans, ospreys, frigate birds, and large marauding gulls. The larger fish have a slightly bluish green cast to the upper back, and all have the ability to camouflage themselves against different backgrounds. The bonefish has a protruding snout that juts out over its lower jaw, forming a mouth that can suck up prey from the bottom. When seen from above against a weedy bottom, the bonefish has a series of dark streaks between rows of scales, making it extremely difficult to see. These bars or lines seem to disappear when the fish is over a white sand or coral marl bottom. In addition, the bonefish has an almost invisible lateral line that picks up the slightest vibrations on the flats, giving it an early-warning system against all predators. Its eyes are covered with a transparent eyelid—much like a pair of goggles—which enables it to see while feeding nose down in cloudy or muddy water.

I, for one, think the bonefish can see *everything* on a flat. It can distinguish different colors. Bright clothing can send it streaking for deep water. It sees well both in bright sunlight and on cloudy days, and I am sure it sees well even at night. It addition to all that protection, the bonefish has an extraordinary sense of smell, which enables it to pick up the scent of its many forms of prey buried in the mud. It can also detect certain odors on flies: gasoline, sunblock, and certain types of insect repellent.

A bonefish can *feel* an angler walking in the sand or mud of a flat. It also picks up the vibration of noise in a flats boat, and you only have to drop an anchor or an oar in a boat and bonefish will spook in all directions. This acute hearing or sense of vibration makes the bonefish extremely wary when in shallow water, where it is vulnerable to enemies.

Until recently, very little has been known about bonefish reproduction and growth rates. The bonefish metamorphoses from a transparent 3-inch eel-like larva that—strangely enough—then shrinks in size. Then a tiny bonefish is formed and begins to grow scales. The fish grows rapidly the first few years, then grows about 2 to 3 inches a year until it is about 6 years old. At that time, the fish is an average of 21 inches long and weighs an average of 5 to 6 pounds.

Marine biologists now tell us that bonefish have lived to an age of about 12 years and may reach lengths in excess of 33 inches, weighing from 14 to 20 pounds at those lengths. The only bonefish I have seen of that size—the one caught in the Yucatan by Will Bauer while I was with him—weighed 14 pounds and was approximately 31 inches long. Though we had a small scale, we had no tape and had to mark its length on a shirt and measure the shirt later. We released the big fish for another lucky angler to catch.

Yucatan 14-pound bonefish, caught by Will Bauer.

Distribution

Bonefish are found on shallow-water flats in tropical seas all over the world. Lately they have been discovered in large numbers on the flats off East Africa in the region of Mozambique. They are also found on flats all over the Pacific and in the Indian Ocean.

For our purposes, there are only a few places where bonefish abound and where fly fishermen can reach them by boat or wading. The best areas are the Bahamas, the Florida Keys, the Los Roques region of Venezuela, Mexico's Yucatan Peninsula, Belize, Honduras, Mozambique, Cuba, Puerto Rico, the Cayman Islands, and Christmas Island in the Pacific. Though some bonefish have been discovered in Australia, not enough have been seen in any one area to establish a fishery.

The bonefish has a lot of local names, but to those of us who fish the Caribbean and Yucatan, it is referred to as *macabi*. In Central and South America it is sometimes called *raton,* or ratfish. In Africa it is referred to as either *ikondo* or *kpole,* and in Hawaii—where it is found only in deep water because there are no flats there—it is called *o'io*.

PERMIT

The Atlantic permit *(Trachinotus falcatus)* is a member of the family Carangidae (the pompano family) and has a number of relatives. The permit is sometimes referred to as the great pompano and, when young, the round pompano. It has a number of local names in the western

Author with a big permit he caught and released on the flats at Guanaja, Honduras.

Caribbean but is generally known as *palometa* to the locals of whatever Spanish-speaking country you're fishing in.

Nobody really knows where the name *permit* came from. I suspect the Spanish name for the fish, when corrupted or said rapidly by English-speaking foreigners, sounded a bit like the word *permit*. I also suspect that that is what it came to be known as by English-speaking residents of such places as the Cayman Islands, Honduras, Belize, and the rest of the Caribbean and the Bahamas.

The all-tackle record for permit—caught in Florida—is 51 pounds, 8 ounces. The fly-rod record is held by Del Brown: a 41-pound, 8-ounce fish caught in Key West, Florida, in 1986. But another, caught by Winston

Moore in Ascencion Bay, Yucatan, was measured, photographed, and released. By using a formula for weight based on length and girth, Moore's fish was estimated to have weighed 44 pounds.

Young permit are either all silver or all dark. Like bonefish, they can change color to blend with their background. Larger fish are usually blue-gray on the back, with the sides and belly silver. There are no black spots or bars on the sides of our Atlantic permit. Permit can best be spotted in the water by the black dorsal fin and black forked tail. Some individuals have an orange or yellow tinge to the anal or pelvic fin area.

Most of what we know scientifically has been gleaned from a study done in the Florida Keys by three

Swimming permit. (Credit: Cam Siegler)

fisheries biologists: Roy Crabtree, Derke Snodgrass, and Peter B. Hood. The study—"Age, Growth, and Reproduction of Permit *(Trachinotus falcatus)* in Florida Water, 1998"—saw 530 permit (291 from the lower Keys and 258 from the Tampa Bay area) sexed and aged from thin-sectioned otoliths (calcareous concretions in the inner ear).

One of the findings that I found somewhat astounding was that permit reach a maximum age of *at least 24 years.* Growth of the permit in the study was found to be rapid until the age of 5 years; then it slowed considerably.

It was found that permit in the waters of the middle and lower Florida Keys spawned in the late spring and summer over reefs at a depth of 40 to 50 feet. Until the study, nobody knew exactly where permit spawned. Many thought it occurred far out to sea.

In the Florida Keys, permit were in danger of being overfished commercially in the 1990s. Commercial fishing yielded 200,000 pounds in 1991, then decreased to about 50,000 pounds in 1995. Current regulations on this great game fish now include a 10-inch minimum and a 20-inch maximum length size limit on both recreational and commercial catches. Recreational anglers are now allowed a ten-fish daily limit and one fish longer than 20 inches, but most fly fishermen release their catch.

Estimate ages of 276 permit studied ranged from 1 year old and 4 inches long to 24 years old and 34 inches long. One marine scientist (Robins) reported in 1992 that permit can reach 44 inches in length and weigh more than 50 pounds, so it is possible that permit may live longer than the 24 years found in the sample tested by the Marine Institute group.

Research also indicates that one sample of lower Keys permit spawned in May to June, whereas other samples of permit in the Tampa Bay area spawned a bit earlier: April to June. It was also found that permit spawned in schools. This is what the scientists refer to as *multiple beach spawning.*

The permit, like the bonefish, spends part of each day in deep water, usually at low tide. It then moves back to the flats on the incoming tide to feed. It behaves much like the bonefish except that it has to wait longer to feed—until the water is deep enough to accommodate its deeper body.

Permit travel in small schools for the most part, although they occasionally feed alone or in pairs. Large schools numbering thousands of fish have been seen in the Florida Keys. When the permit feeds, it "tails" much like a bonefish, its large, black, forked tail in the air and its nose rooting in the bottom. Unlike bonefish, feeding permit do not produce the "mud" typically made by bottom-feeding bonefish schools in deeper water. However, they will sometimes leave small puffs of sand or mud while feeding on the flats.

The permit is a sight feeder, although it may depend somewhat on its keen sense of smell. With its huge, highly specialized eyes, it has marvelous vision. It can spot enemies like barracuda, sharks, man, or boats from a long way off and spooks quickly at any movement. The flash of sunlight on a leader or fly line can send it streaking for deeper water. It will also flee from the shadow of a passing gull, osprey, or pelican.

Although the permit has excellent eyesight while at rest or while swimming, when it's in a feeding position—with tail up and nose on the bottom—its vision is restricted to only a few square inches on the bottom, just ahead of its nose. Consequently, the fish can't see flies cast anywhere outside that small area. This has probably contributed to the generally accepted belief that permit ignore flies.

An imitation crab fly can take a permit if it is properly fished: cast ahead of a swimming permit, then allowed to sink to the bottom and left still, with perhaps just a twitch of movement. This probably works because the permit's favorite food is the crab. Upon seeing a permit approaching, a crab will dive for the bottom and quickly begin to dig into the sand. It will not try to outswim a permit, sensing that would be futile.

A permit can crush quite large objects, including lobsters, clams, oysters, and even conch shells. Australian permit (*Trachinotus blochi*) are called snubnose darts and oystercatchers. Dr. Gordon Hill of Big Pine Key, Florida—a recognized expert on both permit and bonefish who has dissected permit—says the permit has the most enormous rib bones of any fish he knows of. "It is what gives the permit the ability to crush large, hard prey," he says, "and also to let it suck large crabs and things from burrows in the sand—like a large bellows."

I tried for years to find out exactly how a permit crushes its prey. I knew it didn't have the same sort of

Crab fly cast to a tailing permit in Belize.

crushers that a bonefish does, but I couldn't determine exactly how the fish smashed big conch shells and oysters so easily—until Derke Snodgrass of the Florida Marine Research Institute wrote me with his findings in October 1999.

> I worked with Roy [Crabtree] collecting specimens for the study we conducted on permit and several other studies. In doing this, I dissected several hundreds of permit and can answer some of your questions.
>
> As you noted in your letter, the crushing plates on the tongue and roof of the mouth in the bonefish are well developed. That is not the case with permit. It is thought that they crush their prey initially in their

Close-up photo showing extraordinary width of permit rib. (Credit: Dr. Gordon Hill)

throat. They have very strong, recurved plates there that do the initial breakage. Most of the crushing takes place, though, in the intestines. They always have large amounts of hard shell particles filling their intestines. It is here that most of the crushing and digestion takes place.

Of all the stomachs I went through, there were not *any* that did not have an intestine filled with shell particles. It is assumed that they pick this up from deposits on the bottom and not from the items they consume as nutritional sources.

From all that constant rooting on the bottom among hard and sharp shells, the permit's lips are the consistency of a tough rubber tire. It is necessary to set a fly hook firmly to make sure it penetrates.

Crab fly stuck in rubbery lips of small permit. Fish was released.

Distribution

Permit are found all up and down the Atlantic coast, from the mid-Atlantic states to Brazil. They are particularly numerous off South Florida, notably the Florida Keys. The scientific books have a Pacific permit listed *(Trachinotus kennedyi)*, but neither I—nor any of my many permit fly-fishing friends—have ever heard of anyone catching one on rod and reel.

There are a lot of permit in the Bahamas, but no large concentrations in one area. If I had to recommend a spot in the Bahamas, I would say that Bimini and the area just to the east of Deepwater Cay hold the biggest concentrations of permit, but they can also be found off Andros Island and some of the outer islands.

There are permit in much of the Caribbean—in places like Puerto Rico and the Cayman Islands—but not in the concentrations found in the Florida Keys, the Bahamas, the Yucatan, and Belize.

I went to Australia in both 1998 and 2000 and found permit both times. Their big permit *(Trachinotus blochi)* looks much like our Atlantic permit, but many have yellowish dorsal fins and tails. I have yet to catch one, but I have seen a number, especially off the west coast of the Cape York Peninsula in extreme northeast Australia. I did catch three of the smaller cousins of the bigger permit—ones they call the swallowtail dart *(Trachinotus botla)*—which run to about 24 inches long. The swallowtail dart acts just like its larger cousins and is difficult to catch on the flats—though I did take mine on a chartreuse-colored Clouser Minnow fly.

Some of my Australian fly-fishing friends tell me permit may be found in many areas of the Pacific—particularly in New Guinea and the Solomon Islands.

CHAPTER 2

BONEFISH AND PERMIT HABITAT

Most bonefish habitat is basically the same: long stretches of mud, sand, or coral marl flats interspersed with mangrove trees, the bottom sometimes covered with a variety of marine plants. However, in many places—such as Hawaii, Bermuda, and East Africa—bonefish live much of their lives in deep water.

For our purposes, most fly fishermen (and light-tackle anglers) are really only interested in one species of bonefish *(Albula vulpes),* which inhabits the flats of

Ideal bonefish and permit habitat.

tropical seas worldwide. On some flats, there are deep channels, holes, and depressions within the mangroves where some bonefish may decide to stay even after the tide has gone out. They can be caught in these deep holes and channels with sinking or sink-tip lines and weighted flies, but I, personally, never considered that method very sporting—any more than I do dredging a deep-running fly through a bonefish mud in deep water. I feel that fly fishing for both bonefish and permit should be sight fishing—seeing the fish first, then casting to it. In the Yucatan—and in some places in the Bahamas—there are deep "blue holes," openings into underground caves in limestone. Sometimes—particularly in areas like Espiritu Santo Bay in the Yucatan—

Poling for bonefish in the Yucatan.

FLY FISHING FOR BONEFISH AND PERMIT

bonefish can be found near the surface of these big holes and, occasionally, will take a fly.

But most bonefish and permit leave the flats at low tide and head for the deeper water near reefs or into deep channels, only to appear on the flats again on the incoming tide. Nobody really seems to know exactly where bonefish spawn, although Dick Brown, in his excellent book *Bonefish,* writes:

> But we still do not know where and when the bonefish's spawning takes place and where the earliest stages of its life begins. Researchers offer two theories. One holds that bonefish spawn inshore during high tides, then currents and tides take the eggs offshore. Many weeks later as the larva develops, it returns to the shallows where it metamorphoses into a juvenile fish.
>
> A second theory says that bonefish spawn offshore, in relatively deep water. The larva is then carried inshore to the shallows where it metamorphoses into a juvenile.

I don't know where bonefish spawn any more than the next fisherman. The experts do know, however, where permit spawn, as I explained in the previous chapter.

Every bonefish fly fisherman and every guide I know has his own theories—and they're seldom based on scientific research. But we do observe bonefish behavior. A. J. McClane, longtime fishing editor of *Field*

The late A. J. McClane with a Bahama bonefish.

& *Stream* and the editor of *McClane's New Standard Fishing Encyclopedia,* did a lot of fly fishing and research on bonefish and permit in the Bahamas. He told me he had seen what he considered schools of spawning bonefish on the flats near Deepwater Cay in April and May and that they were performing what he considered a "daisy chain" circling motion—a ritual tarpon do while spawning in shallow water.

I have never seen that happen on the flats, but while fishing at the island of Guanaja in the Bay Islands of Honduras one spring with veteran guide and friend Robert Hyde, we did see something unusual. We came upon a school of about thirty to forty large bonefish (in the 8- to 10-pound category) quietly circling in the clear depths of a lagoon surrounded by mangroves. The lagoon was approximately 15 to 20 feet deep. Still, the bonefish were not concerned with our boat, which constantly passed above them. They were not interested in our flies, but continued in their slow circles. Robert, who was born on Guanaja and whose opinions on bonefish and permit behavior I greatly treasure, said the bonefish were "courtin'." That was proof enough for me that at least *those* bonefish were ready to spawn in inshore water.

I have noticed that bonefish on a grassy flat seem to select their prey more than those over sand. On a grassy flat, bonefish will pick out individual items—such as shrimp and clams—whereas on a sandy bottom, bonefish do a lot more rooting and seem to be taking whatever they can find.

I have no logical explanation why bonefish and permit seem to prefer certain flats over others. They look exactly the same to me—miles of the same type of bottom. But local guides say certain flats contain lots more of the kind of food these fish prefer. That makes sense. Robert Hyde once told me permit like certain flats better because they have escape routes they know well and can use in emergencies. That also makes a lot of sense.

Bonefish leave signs that they have been feeding on a flat. Permit really don't leave that many signs. Bonefish leave small, cone-shaped holes in the sand or mud where they have been rooting. An expert can tell what sort of prey they have been after. Lots of pyramid-shaped piles of sand or mud indicate there are mantis shrimp or burrowing urchins on the flat. Small bullet-like holes mean there are clams and shrimp on the bottom, and debris mounds show that crabs have been burrowing.

Although it is very hard to see them over a dark, grassy bottom, bonefish feed on grassy bottoms more than anywhere else. There they can find an assortment of prey they want while they find concealment from predators. Their natural camouflage makes them almost impossible to see over grass. If grassy flats are abundant and if that is where the bonefish are, it is important to remember that almost all their prey species have adapted to the grass background and are the same color. Casting flies the same dark shade makes a lot of sense. Bright-colored flies against such a background tend to spook fish rather than attract them. The same can be said for flies over a white, sandy bottom. White or pink flies fished over glaring white sand take a lot more bonefish than dark-colored flies.

The feeding habitat of permit is basically the same as the bonefish—both grassy and sandy flats—but permit tend to feed more in rocky areas because their favorite food—crabs—cling to and live under such structure.

When not on the flats, permit may be found any-where in deep water. They like to hover around sunken wrecks because of the preponderance of crabs, shrimp, and lobsters that gather there. Also, they cruise along the face of reefs, looking for crabs and other forms of marine life that live there. Divers have told me they see schools of permit close to reefs whenever they go there. Sometimes schools of permit will be seen in the depths simply floating quietly instead of swimming. That is true of a spot called the Elbow, close to a reef on the southern tip of Turneffe Island in Belize. Big-game fishermen have also told me they have seen schools of permit floating close to the surface of the ocean, quite far from shore.

CHAPTER 3

FEEDING HABITS

WHAT BONEFISH EAT

Probably 98 percent of what bonefish eat is what they find on the flats. The other 2 percent, mostly small baitfish, is consumed in the depths.

I learned much from fishing with the late A. J. Mc-Clane, who was constantly searching the flats for more knowledge about both bonefish and permit. A. J. told me once that bonefish and permit will both eat lobsters—not only the regular spiny lobster of the region, but also the smaller slipper lobster, which has no antennae. A. J. was constantly cutting open the stomachs of bonefish (for research on his encyclopedia) in the Ba-

Sand crab, favorite food of the permit.

hamas to determine what they had been eating. He once told me that almost 20 percent of the diet of both bonefish and permit that he had studied in the Bahamas was comprised of mantis shrimp. At the time (the early 1970s), I wasn't that interested in the diet of such fish, and so I forgot it—until almost 25 years later, when I found mantis shrimp were a major prey food for permit and bonefish in the Yucatan and Belize.

A. J. also told me that bonefish ate other fish on the flats, but I was such a novice know-it-all about saltwater fly fishing that I didn't believe him—at least not until his wife, Patti (in the presence of Bing McClelland, A. J., and me), caught a 6-pound bonefish at Cat Cay on a spinning rod with a 6-inch-long, yellow, floating Zaragosa plug, festooned with three sets of gang hooks.

"Bonefish will eat damn near anything when they're really hungry," he said, grinning at me.

Crabs

Crabs make up a large percentage of what the sleek game fish manage to dig out of the sand and mud. Crabs crawl out of their holes when the tide is out and forage for food on the wet surface of the sand or mud flats. When the tide inundates these flats, the crabs are quickly forced underground. Bonefish smell them under the surface and either root them up with their snouts or suck them from their burrows.

These small crabs vary over much of the world, but those in the Bahamas, Florida Keys, and Caribbean are

A big bonefish taken on a Velcro crab fly.

very similar. The common blue crab is found all over this region, as are spider crabs, green reef crabs, the various swimming crabs, fiddler crabs, and stone or mud crabs. Dozens of different hermit crabs are found mostly on the land, after taking over abandoned snail and small conch shells, but some do fall into the water from trees they climb, and some get washed out by tides and are crushed as food by bonefish.

There are all sorts of other crabs that make up the diet of the bonefish, among them the rough-clawed porcelain crab, spotted porcelain crab, purse crab, shamefaced or box crab, common coral crab, gall crab, small reef crab (when it is washed off rocks by waves), and urchin crab.

Mollusks

Of all the critters that bonefish eat, none are as uninteresting to we saltwater fly fishermen as the mollusks: snails, clams, octopods, and squid. Although we do have a chance of tying flies to imitate the small squid (that is, the Squimp fly), I don't know of any fly imitation of snails, limpets, sea slugs, clams, oysters, or mussels, even though we know bonefish eat all these members of the phylum Mollusca.

Concerning the octopods, I have seen any number of small octopuses under rocks on the flats and am sure bonefish eat the small ones. I would be interested in seeing an imitation of that creature.

Shrimp

But when it comes to the shrimp (Penaeidae), we have enough individuals to keep a fly tier busy forever. The

A small octopus on the flat.

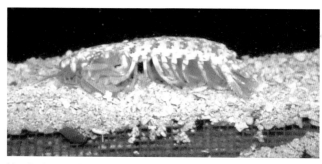

Mantis shrimp. (Credit: Carl Richards)

flats abound in all sorts of shrimp, from the big predaceous golden mantis and green mantis shrimp to the tiny bumblebee shrimp that is found hiding in weed beds.

Nobody but a marine biologist could name half the shrimp that bonefish feed on. They come in a wide range of sizes, but all can be found from the rocks and coral of the reef across the flats and up to the sandy shore of mangrove islands.

The biggest individuals are the white, pink, and brown shrimp, which can grow to a length of 6 to 8 inches. The mantis shrimp—the golden mantis and the green mantis—can be 3 to 4 inches long or bigger and have the ability to slice their prey. The green mantis shrimp, for example, is called *thumb buster,* for obvious reasons. It took most of us saltwater fly fishermen a long time to realize that the mantis shrimp are a major portion of the bonefish diet because both are nocturnal feeders on the flats and hide in burrows all day. Most bonefish fly fishermen—of my acquaintance anyway—can be found in the flats resort bar at night rather than wading the tropical flats in the darkness looking for bonefish food.

Among the many medium-sized and small shrimp that bonefish eat are watchman shrimp, snapping shrimp, sponge shrimp, red cleaning shrimp, Pederson's cleaning shrimp, arrow shrimp, grass shrimp, and bumblebee shrimp.

Almost all of these creatures are distinctively shaped, looking much like water insects. They move forward slowly by using their small paddlelike legs, but swim backward rapidly in a series of short jerks. Most shrimp feed at night and burrow into the sand or mud, or hide in dense weeds, during the day. Shrimp

Bonefish love mantis shrimp—and mantis shrimp flies.

are not difficult to imitate, and there are dozens of excellent shrimp flies available to the fly fisherman.

Urchins

Of the echinoderms (sea stars, brittle or serpent stars, sea cucumbers, sea urchins, sea lilies, and feather stars), the only one I suspect bonefish eat is the sea urchin—that spiny black creature of the flats. Any number of guides—from the Bahamas to Belize—have told me they have seen both bonefish and permit tip up and "tail" over black sea urchins while eating them. Having had sea urchin spines penetrate wading shoes, I'll believe they eat urchins when I see it!

Rays

When it comes to the rays of the flats (of the order Rajiormes), I doubt that bonefish bother the smaller individuals, but I have no proof of that. I do know that the large bonefish sometimes stay quite close to both the common stingray and the eagle ray when churning up the bottom of a flat in search of food. Both bonefish and permit will follow close behind these rays when they are feeding, and a veteran guide will caution a fly fisherman to look carefully behind these curious creatures.

Baitfish

When it comes to the small fish that may become food for bonefish, there are any number of candidates. Per-

The original "Nasty Charlie" bonefish fly invented by Bob Nauheim.

haps the most famous bonefish fly ever devised was created by Bob Nauheim back in the early 1970s on Andros Island in the Bahamas when he and guide Charlie Smith tied up a fly to imitate the glass minnow. It was first called the Nasty Charlie, but later became the Crazy Charlie when carried in the Orvis catalog by Leigh Perkins. It has scores of imitators and has caught bonefish all over the world.

When hungry, a bonefish will eat any small fish it can catch on the flats. That includes the fry of a whole lot of species. There are millions of tiny grunts, snappers, eels, toadfish, gobies, herrings, anchovies, needlefish, half-beaks or ballyhoo, hardhead silversides, remoras, jacks, porgies, drums, mojarras, and Lord knows how many more juvenile forms of fish on the flats that a bonefish can catch and eat. The various colors and sizes of the popular Crazy Charlie fly probably imitate 90 percent of them!

Modern Crazy Charlie bonefish fly.

Worms

A. J. McClane used to tell me that I wouldn't believe the number of marine worms bonefish dig out of the flats. He dug a bunch out of the mud to show me—big, ugly tube worms and a bunch of smaller, almost invisible, transparent worms he had scientific names for, but which I have forgotten.

Bonefish root worms out of the mud and sand. These creatures make up a good portion of their diet. The only problem we have as fly fishermen is that it is very difficult construct a fly to imitate a worm. Ingenious saltwater fly fishermen have done it, however. One of the great examples is the marvelous palolo worm fly tied in the Florida Keys to imitate a worm that hatches each spring and which tarpon take off the surface like trout taking mayflies.

Some of the few successful bonefish worm flies I know of are the Mauna Worm Fly imitation tied for bonefish at Christmas Island in the Pacific; a very ef-

The "Pop" Hill bonefish fly.

fective, spare, monobodied fly tied by the late Dr. "Pop" Hill of the Florida Keys, called the Pop Hill Special; and a sparse, thin plastic worm tube fly, called the Tube Fly, tied by Bonnie Beall.

All these flies make an effort to imitate such marine worms as fanworms, mudworms, threadworms, sand-worms, tube worms, Christmas tree worms, and long-tentacled worms—a major portion of the bonefish diet.

WHAT PERMIT EAT

Permit—as much as bonefish—are what we call op-portunistic feeders. In other words, they will eat just about anything edible they come across on the flats.

With a few exceptions, permit eat the same flats prey over almost all of their range. I am certain the Australian permit eat a different diet from our Atlantic permit, but there is not that much variance in diet between the fish in the Bahamas, the Florida Keys, Jamaica, Puerto Rico, the Yucatan, and Belize.

And although we think we know the diet of permit, we are constantly being surprised. I was fishing with David Westby, one of the great guides of Belize, a few years ago, and we were leaning against a flats boat eating lunch.

"About all we use for these fish are crab flies," I said. "David, there must be *something* else these guys eat on a regular basis."

"Oh yeah, mon," David said casually. "I see them chasin' mantis shrimp all the time."

"Mantis shrimp?" I asked. "How come I never see them chasing them?"

"Two reasons," David said, simply. "You don't know what a mantis shrimp looks like, and they only come out at night."

I stared at him. "Then how come *you* see them?"

"Mon," David said, "I *born* here."

He was absolutely right, and it was as simple as that.

It took about 3 months for me to obtain photos of a mantis shrimp, and it was probably another 3 months before David, his brother Lincoln, Will Bauer, and I came up with two versions of the mantis shrimp fly. Both are very effective at taking permit. It is the only fly I know of that permit will *chase* in the shallow water of a flat.

But that experience taught me a lesson and illustrates a point: There are probably a lot of nocturnal creatures on the flats that serve as both bonefish and

Will Bauer's Mantis Shrimp fly.

permit food, but we hardly ever see them. The mantis shrimp digs into its burrow when the sun comes up, and both bonefish and permit smell them, root them out, and chase them. The vast majority of saltwater fly fishermen never see these encounters.

Like the bonefish diet, the food of the permit can be divided into groups: shrimp, crabs, fish, worms, and clams. In the fish category, we can include such critters as the spiny-skinned brittle stars (Ophiuroodae) and the common sea urchin (Echinoidae). I have never seen permit eat either one, but local guides tell me they do.

I have never seen permit crush and eat oysters either, but my Australian guide friends tell me the Australian permit *(Trachinotus blochi)* is detested by the local oystermen for this practice and is actually called the oystercatcher.

Shrimp

In our hemisphere, it is safe to say that the permit feeds on about every species of shrimp there is,
from the common shrimp (Penaeidae)—which includes the pink, brown, and spotted shrimp—to the
more exotic green, golden, and rock mantis shrimp
(Squillidae). It also eats various members of the snapping shrimp family (Alpheidae): the short-clawed sponge
shrimp, long-clawed sponge shrimp, banded snapping shrimp, red snapping shrimp, and common snapping shrimp.

And although the various smaller shrimp—such as
the arrow shrimp, red-backed cleaning shrimp, bumblebee shrimp, and grass shrimp—average 2 inches
long, they would certainly interest permit.

Crabs

Of the crabs, a permit will eat any it can find—even the
big ones. For years I thought permit ate only the small
ones (which is why we tie small crab flies), but I was
fishing with that excellent guide, Robert Hyde, on
the island of Guanaja in Honduras one day and asked
him what size crabs were best for our flies. He hefted
several of my crab flies—tied on 1/0 and 2/0 stainless steel hooks—then began to push the skiff toward
the nearby shore. While I sat in the boat, he rummaged
about in the thick mangrove bushes and sea-grape trees.

In a moment he came back with several large, dark
red land crabs wrapped in a red bandanna. The biggest
was at least 6 inches wide. Robert broke off its claws

A big sand crab—but not too big for permit.

and reached for a spinning rod in the stern of the boat. He impaled a 4/0 hook through a hole in one edge of the big crab's shell.

"I'll show you," was all he said.

We had poled the boat along the shore for about 20 minutes before Robert shoved the push-pole into the sand and handed me the spinning rod, the big crab dangling from the tip on 20-pound mono. He pointed toward the shore.

"See those permit?" he asked as I squinted. "Right next to that big log—three of them, right close to the bank."

I finally nodded.

"Throw that crab as close to them as you can," he said.

"You're crazy!" I said. "It'll spook the hell out of them."

"Go ahead," Robert said. "Cast it."

To my credit, I made a great cast—landing the big crab about 6 to 8 feet to the right of the fish. The crab landed in the quiet, shallow water with a big splash. The permit closest to it immediately streaked for the crab and seized it. I set the hook by instinct, and the fish was hooked. The other two thrashed away toward deeper water while my hooked permit streaked off to our right, for the depths.

"He took it!" I shouted, raising the rod high over my head.

"Sure, he took it," Robert said calmly. "These big land crabs fall in the water all the time."

It took about 10 minutes to bring the approximately 12-pound permit into the boat—where we released it. I handed the spinning rod back to Robert.

"I'll be damned," I said.

"Permit eat small crabs too," he said, grinning.

The hermit crabs of the species *(paguristes)* are the little critters that take over abandoned conch and snail shells and live on land. They climb trees and bushes and frequently fall into the shallow water, where they are eaten by both permit and bonefish.

Permit also like the big, common blue crab (Portunidae)—as big as it is—and a whole bunch of the same species of swimming crabs, which we generally call sand crabs. They are also fond of the mud crabs (Xanthidae), which include the little black-tipped mud crab and the stone crab—much appreciated by gourmets.

Even the spider crabs (Majidae)—as ugly as they are—are eaten by permit. Permit also suck the green reef crab from the crevasses in the coral and enjoy the spotted and rough-clawed porcelain crabs when they find them. There is hardly a crab a permit will not eat.

Fish and Worms

I have been told that permit will eat baitfish in deep water, and I am sure that is true. They will also catch small fish on the flats, and any small grunt, toadfish, gobie, snapper, or small eel that fails to spot a feeding permit in time will end up as a meal.

All sorts of marine worms also fall prey to searching permit. Anyone who has seen a big permit feeding on a flat—thrashing about in the shallow water, its huge, black, forked tail waving in the air as it throws mud and sand in all directions—knows it is a fierce feeder. It simply isn't selective. Permit that root in the mud or sand will produce fanworms, mudworms, threadworms, sandworms, big tube worms (Onuphidae), and long-tentacled worms.

Both the star and sea urchin—although not fish—interest permit. Permit will also closely follow rays as they churn across a shallow flat and leave a trail of mud and sand in their wake. Cast a fly into the muddy water behind the ray, and permit will think it is a crab disturbed by the digging.

Clams

Trying to categorize all the clams dug up by rooting permit would take a marine biologist all day to chronicle.

On the typical flat, some of them would include the tellins (Tellinidae); both the Caribbean and the candy-stick (Lucinidae); and the three-ridged, the Pennsylvania, the tiger, and the costate lucines.

Permit do not make the huge muds that bonefish schools do when they bottom feed. Instead, permit leave slight depressions and holes in the bottom. It is a sure sign they have been there.

CHAPTER 4

FINDING BONEFISH AND PERMIT
(AND HOW TO SEE THEM)

The habitat of bonefish and permit is virtually the same: flats inside reefs that are either bordering coastal shores or are inland, and vast shallows dotted with mangrove *(Rhizophora mangle)*–covered islands. Although bonefish and permit sometimes feed in the

A typical permit flat.

deep water outside the reefs and perhaps in the deeper channels inland, that does not concern us much as salt-water fly fishermen. We like to be able to see our prey in order to cast flies to it, so we are mostly concerned with the shallow-water habitat of both game fish.

This shallow-water habitat can be either somewhat-barren-looking sand, coral-bottom flats, or flats mostly covered by turtle grass *(Thalassia testudinum)*. Some minor grasses—such as shoal grass—grow closer to shore, but turtle grass is where we find the small fish that make up the daily diet of both bonefish and permit.

And although those glaring white flats may look stark and barren to the casual observer, much of the food sought by bonefish and permit is buried in the soft bottom, where it may be rooted out.

Bonefish and permit may feed together on the same flat. On a number of occasions, I have come across schools of feeding bonefish—usually on an incoming or high tide—with several small groups of permit and some singles busily tailing in the shallow water. That doesn't happen often, but because they eat the same type of food, it is bound to occur now and then. It is a sight to gladden the heart and speed the pulse of any fly fisherman!

It takes some time to learn how to see bonefish. They are extremely difficult for the beginner to see. Bonefish live in a world of bright, ever-changing backgrounds, in which even a stationary, solid-colored object seems to be moving at times. The bonefish is covered with several hundred tiny, mirrorlike, overlapping scales that reflect light in all directions, making

A bonefish suspended over a turtle grass bottom.

the fish almost invisible under most conditions. At first, you have to learn to see the *shadow* of the fish rather than the fish. Later, as you become accustomed to looking at these fish, you become more adept at seeing them.

Bonefish are quite visible when they tail in shallow water: Their silvery tails reflect flashes of sunlight when they protrude above the surface. The other way they become visible—or at least their *presence* becomes visible—is when they are moving as a school in shallow water. The surface becomes rippled above them. Guides refer to this as "shaky" or "nervous" water. Larger single bonefish, or pairs, do not cause such nervous water, but you can sometimes spot them by the V shapes they cause on the surface. Of course, the presence of distinctive "muds" indicates schools of deep-feeding bonefish.

Permit are relatively easy to see—compared with bonefish—although, at times, they too are tough to

Author makes a perfect cast to several feeding permit—which totally ignore the crab fly, as usual. (Credit: Cam Sigler)

spot. In deeper water, a permit can become almost invisible, because its silvery sides also reflect sunlight. The best way to spot this elusive fish is to look for the black, dorsal fin and black, forked tail moving horizontally. Tailing permit are easy to spot, because the black, forked tail is highly visible above the surface, even hundreds of yards away. On the other hand, when wind is rippling the surface, schools of small permit can be almost as hard to see as a bonefish school. Permit schools make nervous water the same as bonefish schools, but schools of large permit make a disturbance on the surface that can be seen from a long way off.

It constantly amazes me the way experienced guides see both bonefish and permit from a distance. It has taken me years to see and understand what these guides are seeing.

My favorite guides—Robert Hyde in Honduras, Lincoln Westby and "Dubs" Young in Belize, and Gil Drake Jr. in the Florida Keys—can spot bonefish and permit when there doesn't seem to be *anything* on the horizon. Robert has taught me one secret: to look at a flat with the thought that any movement at all could be fish. It might be a small school of mullet, it might be a boxfish, it could be a barracuda or a school of small jacks, but at least it is *something,* and it *could* be bonefish or permit.

And after a while, you learn to recognize fish other than bonefish and permit by their distinct behavior. A boxfish "flutters" its tail when feeding nose down and scatters drops of water into the air. A lone barracuda may resemble a resting bonefish, but—on

A permit over a muddy bottom. Note black dorsal fin and black, V-shaped tail.

closer inspection—its tail waves slowly. A queen trig-gerfish, tailing on a distant flat, may speed the heart, but the black tail is blunt, not forked, and tends to stay in the air too long, much like a tailing redfish. Individ-ual fish in a school of mullet in shallow water tend to weave about when swimming. A school of jacks dis-turbs the surface in its own way. It takes time—some-time years—to learn all this!

Seeing undisturbed bonefish in quiet water is un-usual. They stand out quite clearly, and you wonder why they are so difficult to see under most conditions. It is because they are motionless, nose down, and their dark markings show up against the bottom.

Occasionally there will be a school of bonefish at rest against the rocks on the *inside* of a reef. They might be all pointed in the same direction—facing into the slight movement of water coming through the rocks and onto the flat from the sea. Their white bel-lies and dark-barred backs do not blend with the rocky bottom. They seem to be asleep. But cast a fly close to the resting school and the odds are the entire school will churn up the flat and head for deeper water!

Seeing bonefish is one of the most difficult skills to learn. Dick Brown put it well:

> The bonefish's camouflage is so effective that it pre-vents you from catching more than a glimpse of its body, a wisp of its shadow, or the quickest glimmer of its side as its body turns against the sun. If you are going to spot this fish, you have to carry a large

inventory of visual patterns with you, and you must constantly scan the flat for every one of them.

Most of the time, seeing a bonefish requires making a positive match with a known bonefish pattern. You learn the different disguises or "looks" a bonefish adopts. Then you scan the water until you lock into one of these disguises long enough to identify it as a fish. But other times you will see a negative cue—a pattern breaker—that is not part of the background. You catch a glimpse of bonefish color, shape, pattern, and movement that says, "There is something here that does not fit."

I have never heard it put better.

CHAPTER 5

WADING AND POLING, CASTING AND CATCHING

It would be wonderful if all of us were able to find flats where we could wade to both bonefish and permit, but that is seldom the case. Most bonefish and permit flats have soft, muddy bottoms or are in such remote areas that they must be reached by boat. And that boat—be it your own or one belonging to a friend—is costly. Fortunately for a lot of young, athletic flats fishermen, the kayak has come into its own. Lightweight and relatively inexpensive, one can be carried atop a vehicle and transported to areas that have both bonefish and permit—as well as snook, tarpon, and other flats game fish.

There are flats in the Bahamas and Florida Keys that have hard, sandy bottoms. They can be waded, but you must know where they are. Fly shops such as World Wide Sportsman, Inc., in Islamorada, Florida, can tell the novice where to go to find them. However, most fly shops and outfitters would rather recommend a guide who will take fly fishermen—mostly because they know the guides, but also because they don't want to be held liable if some novice fly fisherman gets stuck in the mud or drowns on an unknown flat.

Some lodges on the outlying islands in the Bahamas are perfectly happy to point a fly fisherman toward wadable flats. Needless to say, there are dangers in wading a flat—especially in remote tropical areas. If an angler is not properly equipped with the right footwear, for example, cuts from sharp coral can ruin a day. An ordinary pair of canvas tennis shoes is not enough protection from the spines of sea urchins— those prickly, black invertebrates that dot the bottoms of most flats. The sharp spines will easily penetrate such shoes—as will the toxic spines on tails of rays. There is a real danger of being jabbed by these highly poisonous spines if you are not careful while wading. The spines are not at the tip of the ray's long tail but *on top of the tail at the base—close to the body.*

If you plan to do much flats wading, buy a good pair of thick-soled wading boots with tough uppers. Wear heavy cotton socks to reduce sand blisters. To prevent sand and mud from entering the top of your boots,

A pair of flats wading boots can be invaluable.

A big nurse shark cruising the flat.

wear long trousers with heavy elastic bands about the bottoms of the pant legs. Long pants also prevent annoying bites from sea lice in certain areas. Sea lice are not poisonous but can be a real nuisance.

There is also a danger of sores to the feet from sand inside shoes and boots. Heavy socks can help prevent that. Soft bottoms and strong tides can be a dangerous combination, and care must be taken when wading in such conditions. Also, try not to play hooked bonefish or permit in fairly deep water. The splashes from their struggles may attract sharks and large barracuda, and although there is little danger of a barracuda attack, one might accidentally slice your hand or foot while chasing the hooked fish. Sharks are a different proposition. Bull sharks, in particular, have been known to attack wading anglers in thigh- to waist-deep water.

Several other varieties of sharks must be watched for as well.

One time, I was digging conchs in a soft bottom in the Bahamas, near Deepwater Cay. I was handing a conch up to my guide in the flats boat when he suddenly shouted and yanked me violently into the boat. Just as he did, a 6-foot-long lemon shark streaked into the cloud of mud I had stirred up and circled about violently, searching for the ray it thought had caused all the mud. I hate to think what it might have done to my legs had not the alert guide seen it in time!

I am not trying to frighten anyone away from wading a flat; just use a little common sense. Most flats creatures are far more afraid of you than you are of them and will try to get away when they sight you. However, I'd suggest that you always wade a flat with a friend—not alone.

BONEFISH AND PERMIT ON THE FLY

Bonefish and permit live in similar habitats and feed on the same prey, but they are worlds apart when it comes to the techniques needed to catch them on a fly. Bonefish are not easy to catch on a fly. They are spooky, difficult to see, and smart. Their instincts make them very wary in shallow water, as they are constantly in danger from barracuda and sharks and from ospreys and frigate birds above.

They have learned to fear anglers, be they in boats or wading. In places where they have been heavily

Dark markings on the back of a bonefish taken over a grassy flat.

fished, they are extremely difficult to approach, much less hook. Big bonefish—at such spots as Shell Key, near Islamorada, Florida; the flats at North Bimini; the Middle Bight at Andros Island in the Bahamas; and the flats on Turneffe Island—not only spook when they see bonefish flies, they probably know who tied them!

Even in areas where they don't see that many fly fishermen, the bonefish's natural instinct is to flee at the slightest suggestion of danger. I have seen them flee in a shower of spray from the shadow of a gull passing overhead. Low-flying cormorants will send them off for deep water in a panic. A pelican diving nearby will often cause them to churn up yards of bottom mud. They have good reason to be jittery: Barracuda in pods will sometimes circle their schools like wolves around a flock of sheep and will rip through them like silver arrows, cutting one of them in half as though sliced by a razor. Sharks, sometimes quite big

A nice Turneffe flats bonefish.

ones, will also hunt close to bonefish schools, waiting for careless individuals to stray from the rest. Those sharks, which seem lazy as they weave slowly through the shallows, can move with the speed of light when attacking bonefish. I have lost hooked bonefish to both of these efficient predators.

All of which leaves the bonefish precariously balanced on the sharp edge of danger at all times, so it seldom relaxes. It lives in a world where the slightest movement or vibration might mean threat of death.

Because of this, casting to bonefish must be done very carefully. The flash of sunlight on a leader or line can send the individual or school streaking away. The sound of a leader or line hitting the water can alert them. Any sound in a flats boat—a dropped push-pole, a chain striking the bottom of the boat, a dropped rod and reel, almost any sound—can make them wary.

When wading for bones, be very careful not to step on sticks, rocks, or brittle coral. Bonefish will pick up

Fisherman plays a big Yucatan bonefish.

FLY FISHING FOR BONEFISH AND PERMIT

the vibrations and be gone by the time you begin to cast. Brightly colored clothing will spook them. I always wear neutral shirts and hats—preferably tan—when wading. Bright clothing in a boat also will alert them.

I certainly cannot prove it, but I swear permit see more than bonefish and are far more wary. We can tell what frightens bonefish. There are times when I have no idea why permit spook. I personally believe they have some sort of extrasensory perception that sometimes makes them simply disappear—not quickly spook, but just fade away quietly.

Permit are the most difficult of all flats game fish to cast a fly to. In the first place, they don't often *take* flies—as opposed to bonefish, which seem to like flies at times. When a permit finally takes a fly, it is usually an accident, sort of an afterthought. The only fly I have ever seen a permit deliberately *chase* is the mantis shrimp pattern. My guide friends tell me that's because any mantis shrimp that a permit sees on the flats has just been flushed from a burrow and is moving very rapidly—in quick spurts. They say the permit is acting by instinct when it chases this fly because it knows a mantis shrimp is only going to be there for a few more seconds before it burrows back into the bottom. Bonefish will chase mantis shrimp the same way.

Bonefish will readily take a fly under the best of conditions. There are also days when they will ignore every one cast at them—because of water temperature, barometric pressure, wind-whipped water, or just plain cantankerousness.

Wading for Bonefish

Let's assume a beginner is wading his first bonefish flat somewhere in the Bahamas. What should he look for? Without a guide to point out fish, the novice will have to begin with the basics.

Bonefish are very difficult to see. Their skin is made up of dense, overlapping, shiny scales—much like tiny mirrors—that reflect light and make the fish almost invisible against any background. If there is bright sunlight, look for the fish's shadows on the bottom. Bonefish may be traveling in large schools, small schools, or even as single fish. Look for erratic movement. Bonefish (and permit) seldom remain still for more than a few seconds. They are constantly searching the bottom for food.

If you detect a shadow that remains still, it is probably a barracuda. It could be one of any number of snappers or grunts, but these fish remain close to rocks, sunken logs, or other structure, such as dock pilings. Sometimes needlefish rest on the surface and cast a shadow on the bottom, but bonefish do not stay on the surface. Small tarpon are silver and are often found floating immobile in the shallow water of flats, but remember: Bonefish hardly ever stay still for more than a few seconds. Snook will lie close to mangrove roots in wait for prey, but they too will remain very still for long periods of time.

Yucatan guide holding a boxfish that took a fly.

If you are looking for tailing bonefish, remember that the tail is forked, silver, and—when the fish is feeding nose down—will only wave in the air for a few seconds before the bonefish moves on to feed in another spot.

All this can be discouraging at first, but take heart. After a few sightings, you will become used to the differences in these fish.

If the sky is overcast and there is wind blowing, there is almost nothing I can say that will help locate bonefish or permit—unless by a freak chance you spot tailing fish.

If the surface of the flat is calm, watch for surface movement. Fish moving in shallow water will cause a ripple effect on the surface. This condition (unfortunately) can also be caused by any number of other fish—mullet schools, baitfish, small jacks, needlefish, barracuda—all sorts of fish. But at least the surface movement gives the beginner a chance to get ready. When the commotion turns out to be caused by bonefish or permit, it will have been worth the wait.

If the school of whatever-it-is approaches, stand still if it appears to be approaching. If it seems as if it will pass to the left or right, move *slowly and quietly* in that direction while getting ready to cast.

When it is determined that the fish are bonefish, and moving, cast ahead of the school and strip the fly in short jerks as it settles toward the bottom. Try to make only one backcast, then cast the fly. Line in the air can easily spook bonefish or permit, and the fewer the casts, the better.

If the bonefish or permit stop to feed and tail, cast directly at the closest fish (getting as close as possible) and allow the fly to settle to the bottom. In the case of bonefish, begin to strip. For permit, let the fly settle to the bottom and wait for the fish to discover the fly. If a permit ignores the fly, twitch it slightly to get its attention.

Years ago, when most of us began to learn saltwater fly fishing, we would raise the rod tip immediately and strike with the arm when a bonefish or permit picked up a fly. The fact that it worked is a testament to luck more than skill. As we became more experienced, we learned to strike with the free hand (in the case of right-handers, the left hand holding the loose fly line). The strip-strike is a quick jerk of the free hand backward, setting the hook. Then the fly rod may be raised to take up slack line and let the fish run "on the reel." This is very important in saltwater fly fishing, because these game fish are fast and strong, and holding on to the line after the strike may well break the tippet.

Once the fish is on, hold the rod high overhead to keep the line as much out of the water as possible and away from obstacles such as mangrove roots, small mangrove trees, floating logs, coral heads, and other potential problems. Let the fish wear itself out against the drag of the reel. Don't put too much pressure on until the fish begins to tire and comes close to the boat (or your feet, if you're wading).

There are a few basic rules about casting to bonefish. Never cast into the center of a bonefish school, whether the fish are tailing or not. They will spook. Avoid false-casting over the school. Try to get the fly close to the school or in front of it on the first cast.

When casting to tailing bonefish, try to get the fly close to the side of the school nearest you. If casting to a single tailing bonefish, make sure there are no other fish feeding close to it. Wait until it is head down and tail up, and try to get the fly as close as possible.

When casting to a school of swimming bonefish— or even a single fish—get the fly some distance ahead of the fish and hope they (or it) will pass over your offering. As the fish approach, let the fly settle close to the bottom, then begin to strip it in short jerks. If a fish begins to follow it steadily, speed it up a bit. If it continues to follow the fly but will not take it, sometimes letting the fly settle to the bottom will induce a strike.

I am not a big fan of fly fishing for bonefish in deep water, especially when they are on the bottom and creating big "muds" (because I don't consider it as sporting as casting to fish I see). But sometimes they are not feeding on the flats, and a guide will point to the muddy area.

In this case—and if you want to try for them—you should cast over the muddy area, let the fly sink slowly into the depths, then slowly strip the fly through the mud. This is blind casting and, for my money, a dull way to fish, but it does produce strikes. And once in a while a big bonefish will come out of a mud. What was that about even a blind hog finding the occasional acorn?

A large school of bonefish.

Finding, seeing, and casting to bonefish—even on a bright, sunny day—is not always easy. On a dull, overcast day—with wind and rain—it can be sheer agony. The bonefish are almost impossible to see, they don't feed and tail much under such conditions, and even if they *were* causing nervous water, no one could see it. On a day like this, even I might hope to find a big mud!

PERMIT ON THE FLATS

There is no mistaking a permit on a flat. If it is tailing, you cannot miss that huge, black tail. If it is swim-

A guide getting ready to tail a big bonefish.

ming, the black dorsal and forked tail stand out clearly. Casting to swimming permit requires that the fly be cast far ahead of the fish so that it will be close to or on the bottom by the time the permit see it. *Don't start stripping the crab fly*—no matter how loudly the guide yells, "Strip, strip!" A guide who does this does not know much about permit fly fishing—either that, or it is just perfectly understandable panic on his part.

A crab fly—the only acceptable fly for permit (besides the mantis shrimp fly)—should be left to rest on the bottom as the permit approaches it. Permit take live crabs on the bottom. If the permit begins to swim by the immobile crab fly, the fly could be given a few slight twitches, but not more than an inch each time.

Author with a nice Turneffe Island permit that took a small crab fly.

Small No. 4 hook Stone Crab fly, which works on Turneffe Island permit.

Permit will sometimes turn and take the crab fly. Eighty times out of one hundred, they will totally ignore the crab fly—because that is what permit *do*. Permit fly fishing is the most frustrating fly-fishing sport in the world! Catching Atlantic salmon on a fly is a lead-pipe cinch compared with permit, and salmon are difficult to take on a fly. But that is *why* we fly fish for permit.

As Al McClane used to say, "If they took flies every day, we'd never fish for them."

Those of us who have fly fished for permit over the years consider only those fish caught in shallow water, on the flats, as *legitimately* or fairly caught permit. There are all sorts of reports of permit caught on a fly that don't fall into that category. For instance, I do not consider catching permit over wrecks—by jigging a glistening, Mylar-type streamer fly deep in the midst of chum—catching a permit on a fly. Nor do I condone some other methods, such as chumming with small

Guide tails a big permit in Ascencion Bay, Yucatan.

live crabs or dead minnows thrown into deep holes or channels, and then stripping crab flies deep in the chum.

That is why I am not enamored with stripping flies through muds for bonefish. Fly fishing for both bonefish and permit should be sight fishing—casting flies at fish we can *see*.

Landing Fish

It is preferable to use a long-handled landing net to scoop up bonefish while fishing from a boat. While wading, you simply have to use your hands and hope for the best. Bonefish are sleek and slippery, but the best grip is just before the tail. Many experienced fly fishermen simply slide a hand beneath the belly and gently lift the fish.

Landing a permit is always a problem. It never really gives up; it makes sudden, strong runs, even when it reaches the boat or the legs of the wader. But if it comes within arm's reach, the narrow spot just ahead of the forked tail is the best place to grab it . . . and *hang on!* A big permit will put up a battle even after being grabbed.

While we are on the subject of grabbing bonefish and permit, why not release all your fish? Most serious fly fishermen do. Even if you think you have a world record, you can photograph it, weigh it, and measure it, and the International Game Fish Association (IGFA) will take your word for it on a world-record application if you have the weight (taken on an IGFA-certified scale) and a photo. Send your scales to the IGFA,

Will Bauer releases a nice Belize permit.

Measuring a permit prior to release.

300 Gulf Stream Way, Dania Beach, FL 33004. There is a nominal charge.

As far as how to measure: The girth of the fish should be measured, and that number squared. The girth is measured just ahead of the dorsal fin. That number is then multiplied by the length, measured from the tip of the nose to the base of the V in the fork of the tail. That number is then divided by 800. The result should give you the weight. Taxidermists are so good today that they can make you an exact duplicate cast of that record fish.

Casting from a Boat

Casting from a boat gives you the advantage of height and better vision. (Given a choice, though, I'd rather wade to both bonefish and permit. I have all that solid ground to stand on when I'm wading, and I can present

Playing an Ascencion Bay bonefish.

a better silhouette against the sky background than in a boat.) Most guides would prefer you stay in the boat, probably because they feel they have better control over the situation, and they certainly can see the prey better from their elevated position. The trouble is that not all guides know how to position a boat to the fly fisherman's best advantage, and when they don't align the boat for a good cast, it is very difficult to present a fly properly. There is also a good chance of accidentally hooking the guide on the backcast.

Experienced professional guides immediately jam the tip of the push-pole into the bottom and swing the bow of the boat so the fly fisherman has nothing behind him to snag the fly. These veteran guides will also see bonefish or permit before the angler does and can give directions that will make it much easier for the angler to spot and cast to the quarry.

Distance and angle from the fly fisherman are vitally important in this sport when seconds count. "Forty feet at 11 o'clock" would be an ideal observation on the part of a good guide—when that is where the fish is. Unfortunately, most bonefish or permit are more likely to be 80 feet away—and moving fast!

If a fly fisherman can cast easily to 50 to 60 feet, he should have no trouble reaching bonefish—and some permit. Those who can cast 80 to 100 feet are in the minority. I know some fly fishermen who can cast an entire 90-foot fly line outside the rod tip, but they are few and far between, and even those experts cannot always do it while casting into the wind. Add a few other factors—a rocking boat, gusting winds, the fly line blowing about the deck around your feet—and the problem becomes compounded.

Casting to bonefish at Guanaja, Honduras.

A stripping basket sometimes helps in keeping fly line unimpeded, but I find them uncomfortable to wear. Keeping a plastic wastebasket at your feet and piling loose line in it is one solution, but the wastebasket keeps getting in the way. If you're standing on the casting platform on the bow of a flats boat, letting the loose line pile up there works fine unless there is a strong wind—in which case the line can blow overboard and cause all sorts of problems. On windy days, I strip my loose line back into the bottom of the boat after making absolutely sure there are no protrusions there—such as cleats, nails, or loose tackle—to snag the line. On windy days, it is probably smarter to keep the line on the reel until needed, but it always seems fish show up suddenly, and you don't have time to strip that line off the reel in time. That is one reason I like to wade and let the line float behind me on the surface.

A lot of veteran saltwater fly fishermen go barefoot while standing on the forward casting platform. This is so they can feel the loose fly line beneath their feet and won't be standing on it when they cast. You always take a chance of getting sunburned feet that way and, personally, I find standing for hours in bare feet tends to make the arches ache and the legs cramp. I'd rather wear a good boat shoe with arch supports and gamble that I won't stand on the line.

Being able to see bonefish and permit a distance away from the boat gives a saltwater fly fisherman a great advantage. I know veteran flats fishermen who regularly see fish before their guides do. A good, wide-brimmed hat helps greatly, or a cap with a long bill. The underside of the cap bill should be a dark color to cut down on glare. Polarized glasses cut down on surface glare and are a must if you are to see fish against a varied background.

The direction of the wind is everything in casting a fly to these wary flats fish. Most of us are right-handed, and wind blowing from our right can be a real problem. The same is true in reverse for left-handed casters. And even the "experts" have problems with wind direction. The late, great Lee Wulff once told me he had a foolproof way to tell whether he had gone to heaven or hell.

"When I wake up and the wind is blowing toward my right shoulder, I'll know immediately," he said wryly.

I hope, where he is now, the wind is always blowing from his left.

There are those—like some of my tarpon guide friends who have spent a lifetime on the windy flats—who can hurl a big fly right into the teeth of a strong wind, or backhand a big tarpon fly nearly 100 feet with a 12-weight rod. I am not one of them, nor are most fly fishermen I know.

It may be easier to control a hooked bonefish or permit from a boat than while wading because of the increased height and better visibility to see such obstacles as mangrove stalks, mangrove roots, coral outcroppings, and floating debris. But you sometimes sacrifice firm footing for height. I like to step down from the casting platform after hooking a fish and fight it while standing on the bottom deck of the boat.

While standing on the casting platform and waiting to spot bonefish or permit, hold the fly in your non-casting hand. Don't let it trail in the water close to the boat. It is likely to pick up small bits of debris that way (weed, grass, or leaves), or your fly may be neatly cut off by a small barracuda just about the time you spot a feeding permit.

CHAPTER 6

HOW TIDES, WATER TEMPERATURE, AND BAROMETRIC PRESSURE AFFECT BONEFISH AND PERMIT

Generally, both bonefish and permit move in to feed on an incoming tide, swimming in from the deep water to find their favorite foods on the shallow waters of the flats. Perhaps the primary difference between the two game fish is that bonefish will sometimes remain in deep-water areas on the flats, whereas permit like to return to deep water when a tide is out.

Marine scientists have found that bonefish will feed on the entire incoming tide cycle. Sometimes, when there is very little change between high and low tides, they will feed through both tide cycles on any flat that constantly produces food.

I cannot say for certain that permit feed only on the incoming tides in the Florida Keys and Bahamas, but I have done considerable research on this phenomenon in Belize. On the many flats scattered through the deep waters of Belize—from the area of Tobacco Cay to the Plancencia and the Gladden Entrance—permit will consistently come up on these flats on the rising tide. There they will feed voraciously—tailing vigorously on the coral bottom—until the tides go out. When the tide approaches low, it is difficult to find a permit on any of those flats. Experienced guides, such as Lincoln Westby of the Blue Horizon Lodge on Northeast Cay, won't take clients out until the tide starts coming in. They know it would be a waste of time.

Bonefish and permit seem to have the same general likes and dislikes when it comes to water temperature. Dick Brown, author of the excellent book *Fly Fishing for Bonefish* (The Lyons Press, 1993), writes that scientists in the Bahamas have found that larger bonefish can withstand cold longer than smaller bonefish, but have less tolerance for warm water. He cites studies done at Deepwater Cay, where larger bonefish—about 5 pounds—left the flats in months when the water temperature rose above 93 degrees F, whereas smaller bonefish remained. The larger bonefish returned to the flats in months when temperatures dropped to about 73 degrees F.

A permit hooked on a Velcro crab fly.

A. J. McClane—who probably collected more data on bonefish than anyone—noted that bonefish feed most frequently in the 68- to 88-degree-F temperature range. Gordon Hill of Big Pine Key, who probably knows more about Florida Keys permit than any fly fisherman alive, says that Keys permit there are affected by winds—they prefer an east or southeast wind of about 10 knots. According to Hill, neither bonefish nor permit feed well on a west wind. He also says that the best flats temperatures in the Lower Keys are in the 73- to 92-degree-F range. That has also proven to be true in Belize and the Yucatan Peninsula of Mexico. He adds that bonefish and permit do not care for sudden weather changes, which cause both temperature and barometric changes. Hill has caught most of his permit when water temperatures on the flats of the

About-to-be-released permit.

Bonefish sometimes lurk in extremely shallow water just inside reefs.

Keys are in the upper-80- or lower-90-degree range, but he says he has never seen a permit on the flats when the water temperature was 94 degrees F.

I cannot say how many times I have seen bonefish schools lying close against the coral rocks of an outer reef with the wind blowing in from the sea. They are either tailing close to the reefs or lying up against the rocks in only a few inches of water. I can only assume they are feeding on particles of food washed in from the ocean waves and currents. I expect there is a larger variety of food washed in from the sea at the reef than at other inland spots. Permit also like to cruise and feed in those inside waters, just inside reefs. These waters also provide instant escape avenues through the coral heads into deep water.

Tides, which affect the feeding cycles of bonefish as well as permit, are caused by the gravitational pull of the moon. And the moon itself has a decided effect on the feeding habits of both bonefish and permit. I have seen both bonefish and permit tailing on the flats during the full of the moon and on nights on either side of the full moon. It is worth keeping that in mind when planning a trip. Bonefish and permit that have fed all night under a full moon are not likely to be hungry the next day and certainly not the next morning. Other things being equal, a trip planned during the dark phases of the moon should be more productive.

CHAPTER 7

A BRIEF HISTORY OF AMERICAN BONEFISH AND PERMIT FLIES

Unlike trout and salmon flies, which have been around for hundreds of years, bonefish flies have generally been used only since about the late 1940s. Permit flies came along a decade after that, and there were not more than half a dozen flies in use by the late 1960s. It is still a brief history.

BONEFISH FLIES

There were fly fishermen catching bonefish in the Florida Keys as early as the 1920s. Holmes Allen of Miami was reported to have taken the first bonefish on a white "crippled minnow" streamer fly in 1924.

Shortly after that, there were any number of Florida Keys guides and anglers who began experimenting with flies. The late Joe Brooks, fishing editor of *Outdoor Life,* popularized a successful bonefish fly called the Phillips Pink Shrimp. It caught a lot of bonefish. After that, it was every man for himself, and by the 1950s there were scores of bonefish flies in the tackle shops and catalogs.

The most successful bonefish flies imitated shrimp, small baitfish, crabs, or worms, whereas the few permit flies that worked were crude imitations of crabs. A number of permit were caught on bonefish flies, and some still are. Others were caught on tarpon flies—an occurrence nobody can explain.

Many of the first flies cast at bonefish were actually refinements of established freshwater trout flies. Some of them worked, but most got caught in weeds and turtle grass because the hook rode point down.

As a result, fly fishermen such as Bermuda's Pete Perenchief, Miami's Chico Fernandez, and California's Bob Nauheim designed flies like the Horror, the Bonefish Special, and the Nasty Charlie—all of which rode hook up and used a tuft of bucktail riding upright to make them weedless. These flies revolutionized bonefish fly tying and were copied everywhere.

Catalogs and fly shops today advertise hundreds of bonefish flies. Most are variations on the original Nasty Charlie (now called the Crazy Charlie), which was tied by Bob Nauheim and Bahama guide Charlie Smith to imitate a glass minnow. Theoretically, all the flies copied from the Crazy Charlie are imitating small baitfish.

Other modern bonefish flies, like Jim Orthwein's Rubber Band Worm, imitate worms. Other flies—Jim's Goldeneye Shrimp, the Mantis Shrimp, the Pink Shrimp, and dozens more—imitate shrimp.

Small crab flies—like Carl Richards's Green Reef Crab, Jack's Fighting Crab, Peterson's Spawning Crab, the Stone Crab, Will Bauer's Green Wool Crab, the Turneffe Crab, and others—when used on small hooks work well for bonefish.

A lot of bonefish fly fishermen have no idea what an arrow shrimp looks like, but it is part of the steady diet of bonefish. It is a small, sometimes translucent shrimp that is found among the coral and bottom grass of most Florida, Caribbean, and West Indian flats. It feeds on organic material and darts about in such habitat as turtle grass. Like its name, it looks like a small silvery, green, or brown arrowlike shrimp—usually less than an inch long.

To imitate it, tie a very sparse fly—trying for the same colors—without large, beady eyes. I tie mine on a No. 6 Mustad 34007 stainless steel hook. It should be stripped in short, quick jerks not more than a few inches long. This is an excellent "skinny" water fly, as it lands with almost no splash and therefore does not spook bonefish in clear, shallow water. One of the drawbacks of bead-eye Crazy Charlie–type flies is that they tend to spook fish in calm water.

Small, sparse, silvery flies may also be used to imitate the common grass shrimp, which is a transparent,

Author's sparse Arrow Shrimp bonefish flies.

The original Puff The Magic Dragon permit fly, invented by Nat Ragland in the 1960s.

small (usually an inch or less) shrimp that darts among the blades of grass. It is safe to say that very few bonefish fly fishermen today use this type of fly. Most have been convinced that the bead-eye flies work best for bonefish. Having said that, I will admit that many of the bead-eye flies work admirably or they would never have lasted as long as they have.

Some of the great early bead-eye-type flies were the Evil Eye, by George Hommell; the Blue Tail Fly, by Captain Bill Curtis; Bonnie's Evil Eye, by Bonnie Beall; Olch's Florida Shrimp; the Peacock Angel, by Jack Gartside; the Clouser Deep Minnow, by Bob Clouser; and the Puff Fly, by Nat Ragland.

There are hundreds of bonefish flies to choose from; I have chosen some of the most successful flies and keyed them to areas, starting on page 99.

Permit Flies

Permit fly fishing is still in its infancy. I doubt if there are more than a dozen permit flies that deserve the description *successful* (see the box starting on page 106 for my picks). Even the best-known permit flies do not catch permit consistently. No fly does!

The history of permit flies is a short one. The very first flies to catch permit were tarpon and bonefish flies, but anyone who knows permit also knows that catching them on these flies is an accident. I know fly fishermen who have caught permit on tarpon flies, and each one has been astonished when the permit took that fly. It was totally out of character for the permit.

I once met a fly fisherman, a doctor from Chicago, who proudly told me he had caught his first permit the day before on the flats of Guanaja in Honduras. When asked what he caught it on, he proudly showed me a small, brown Crazy Charlie bonefish fly! I don't know why I was so surprised. I keep forgetting I caught my own first permit on a Phillips Pink Shrimp bonefish fly at Cat Cay, more than 30 years ago.

Flies purposely tied to catch permit came out of the Florida Keys in the late 1960s. The first two were Harry Spear's Epoxy Fly and Nat Ragland's Puff Fly (named Puff the Magic Dragon). Both flies caught permit when few other flies did.

A couple of Puff-type flies began to show up in the fly shops, and though I cast them to any number of permit, I never got a take.

I caught my second permit on a fly in the early 1980s at Turneffe Flats in Belize, fishing with the late, great guide Joel Westby. We caught a big 18-pound permit using Spear's Epoxy Fly. It was the only time I ever caught a permit with that fly—but it was memorable!

The original Epoxy Fly, invented by Florida Keys guide Harry Spear.

I don't know what year Del Brown, fishing with Jan Isley, began using the Merkin—a strange-looking yarn fly—but I know George Anderson created the McCrab fly in about 1985. It was a difficult-to-tie deer hair fly that sold for $12. I know because I paid for four of them that year and caught four permit with them at Guanaja the following year.

I have never caught a permit with Del Brown's yarn fly, but many guides in the Florida Keys swear by it and ones like it. Jan Isley went on to guide in the Yucatan's Ascencion Bay area, running the Ascencion Bay Bonefish Club for 9 years. While there, he developed the highly successful Isley's Raghead Permit Fly. It is heavy to cast, but veteran permit fly fishermen, such as Winston Moore, love it and have caught any number of big permit with it. It spawned a host of imitations.

A commercial version of the Puff Fly.

Sometime in the late 1980s, a West Coast fly fisherman named Frank Raspo was with his wife, who was shopping in a ladies' apparel store. Frank noticed that the Velcro Company made small circular and square patches for sewing called Velcro Sticky-Back Coins. He immediately saw the possibilities of using them for permit crab flies and began to experiment with them. In the following few years, he caught a number of permit with the small fly in the Yucatan. It was the beginning of several Velcro crab flies. He showed it to me, and I went on to add two mallard flank feathers to it. It became Jack's Fighting Crab and was picked up by the Orvis catalog. It has caught a lot of permit.

One of the most successful permit crab flies I know of was developed by Californian Will Bauer, who ran a fishing resort in Belize in the 1980s and became fascinated with fly fishing for permit. A very knowledgeable fly fisherman, he began looking at the native crabs on the flats of Belize and found most were small, green

Original Velcro Crab fly, invented by Frank Raspo.

Jack's Fighting Crab fly.

Will Bauer's small, green Belize Permit Crab fly.

Dr. Gordon Hill's Keys permit flies.

crabs about the size a quarter. He tied a small Green Wool Crab Fly and began catching permit. Today, he has caught almost 100 permit using that same fly.

Gordie Hill of Big Pine Key—a veteran permit fly fisherman who is truly an expert on permit behavior—makes up his own permit crab flies of deer hair, feathers, and rubber bands. They are not sold anywhere, but they sure catch permit.

Nat Ragland's original Puff Fly has undergone some modification, but it is still called the Puff and is very successful in the Florida Keys.

Carl Richards, that fine fly tier from Michigan, probably became the first fly fisherman to discover that the mantis shrimp fly he made up caught permit. It is beautifully tied, like all of his creations. In the early 1990s, Will Bauer and I discovered that permit in Belize were fond of the green mantis shrimp. We tied up separate versions of the creature, but both work equally well—in green and in orange spawning color.

A BRIEF HISTORY OF AMERICAN FLIES

Veteran fly tier and saltwater fly fisherman Terry Baird ties up a creation he calls his Hula Shrimp. Orvis carries it in the catalog, and it comes in both bonefish and larger sizes. I caught a 15-pound permit on a green version of the Hula Shrimp while fishing with guide Carmen Hyde from that excellent fishing lodge, the Bayman Bay Club, on the island of Guanaja in Honduras. Both he and I were surprised the permit took it, because I was using the shrimp fly for bonefish.

But the biggest surprise in the past few years is the success of the green mantis shrimp fly for permit. I have caught a number of permit on my version of the fly, mostly in Belize. The mantis shrimp fly is the only fly I know of that permit will *chase*.

Anyone who doubts the success of this fly need only contact Doug Schlink of Angler Adventures in Old Lyme, Connecticut.

Doug was fishing Ascencion Bay in the Yucatan in October 1999 at the venerable Casa Blanca lodge. The weather had been marginal for days, and crab flies had produced no permit takes. Late on the last day of the trip, he and his guide spotted a small school of permit in fairly deep water at the west end of the big bay. The water was too deep for them to easily watch where Doug's crab flies were sinking, and it was difficult to see if the permit were even interested in them.

His guide, Augustine, reached into a shirt pocket and came up with a green mantis shrimp fly.

"Here," he said to Doug. "Use this. You'll catch one."

Doug told me he switched to the mantis shrimp fly, made one cast over the permit school, and *three permit*

Carl Richards's Mantis Shrimp fly. (Credit: Carl Richards)

Terry Baird's Mantis Shrimp fly.

Jack's Mantis Shrimp fly.

Exhausted permit, prior to release. (Credit: Cam Siegler)

chased it on the surface. He caught the lead fish—a permit of about 15 pounds!

I have had the most success in the past few years with my own small crab fly, tied on a No. 4 stainless steel hook. I finally concluded that big crab flies spook permit too easily and consequently switched to smaller crab flies. I tie my fly to imitate the little black-tipped mud crab and the small stone crab, both of which have black-tipped claws. It is much easier to cast in a wind, and it does not make much of a splash when it hits the surface. I had an approximately 40-pound permit take it in Belize while I was fishing with Lincoln Westby, and both Cam Sigler and I have taken some nice permit with it on Turneffe Island in Belize. I call it Jack's Stone Crab.

Nowadays the fly catalogs are filled with all sorts of new bonefish and permit crab flies. I am sure some of them work, but most are just variations on the old tried-and-true patterns.

Jack's Stone Crab Fly.

Go Weedless

There are places—some spots in the Keys and Bahamas, and the flats near Ambergris Cay in Belize—where you need weedless bonefish and permit flies. To my knowledge, fly shops don't sell them weedless, so it is up to the individual fly fisherman to make his own flies weedless.

Bending 20- to 30-pound mono around the hook while making the fly works fine, but I use a different system. I take Sevenstrand stainless steel wire, quite fine (#27 12kg) and lay a short length of it on the hook shank, at the hook eye. With a length sticking out, I wrap the wire tight with mono thread. Then I bend the wire back with small pliers and cut it off just barely ahead of the hook point (see illustrations on pages 96–98). It is strong enough, almost invisible, and keeps the weeds off the hook point.

Stainless steel wire (#27 12kg), to make flies weedless.

Tie short length of wire to hook shank.

Grasp with needle-nosed pliers.

Bend wire up and back.

With cutters, snip wire just ahead of hook point.

Finished weed guard.

THE BEST BONEFISH FLIES FOR THESE DESTINATIONS

Florida Keys

Chico's Bonefish Special—Size 2, 4 ⌐

Pink Crazy Charlie—Size 6, 8 ⌐

Squimp—Size 6
Mantis Shrimp—Size 2, 4
Absolute Flea—Size 4, 6 ⌐

Hula Shrimp—Size 6, 8
Spawning Shrimp—Size 2, 4 ⌐

Crazy Charlie Lead-Eye—Size 6, 8
Deep Water Gotcha—Size 2, 4
Green Weenie—Size 4, 6 ⌐

Bahamas

Rubber Band Worm—Size 2, 4
Crustacean—Size 6, 8 ⌐

Crazy Charlie Lead-Eye—Size 6, 8
Pink Crazy Charlie—Size 6, 8
Chico's Bonefish Special—Size 2, 4
Agent Orange—Size 4, 6 ⌐

Whitlock's Shrimp—Size 2 ⌐

Chico's Snapping Shrimp—Size 2, 4
Spawning Gotcha—Size 6, 8
Bonefish Pearl—Size 4, 6
Mantis Shrimp—Size 2 ⌐

Absolute Flea—Size 2, 4
Bonefish Slider—Size 4, 6
Hula Shrimp—Size 6, 8
Horror—Size 2, 4 ¬

Clouser Minnow—Size 2

Mexican Yucatan/Central America

Bonefish Gotcha—Size 6, 8
Crazy Charlie—Size 4, 6
Bonefish Bitters—Size 2, 4 ¬

Raghead Crab—Size 2
Mantis Shrimp—Size 2, 4
Absolute Flea—Size 4, 6

Arrow Shrimp—Size 6, 8 ⌐

Spawning Shrimp—Size 4, 6
Squimp—Size 6, 8
Mini-Puff—Size 4, 6 ⌐

Epoxy-Backed Shrimp—Size 3 ⌐

Crustacean—Size 4, 6

Venezuela

Chico's Bonefish Special—Size 4, 6
Pink Crazy Charlie—Size 6, 8
Agent Orange—Size 4, 6
Deep Water Gotcha—Size 6, 8 ⌐

Spawning Gotcha—Size 4, 6
Mantis Shrimp—Size 4, 6
Crazy Charlie Lead-Eye—Size 6, 8 ⌐

Rubber Band Worm—Size 4, 6
Hula Shrimp—Size 2, 4 ⌐

Bonefish Slider—Size 6, 8 ⌐

Christmas Island

Pink Crazy Charlie—Size 4, 6, 8
Crazy Charlie Lead-Eye—Size 4, 6, 8
Bonefish Slider—Size 4, 6
Squimp—Size 4, 6, 8 ⌐

Deep Water Gotcha—Size 4, 6
Spawning Gotcha—Size 6, 8

Clouser Minnow—Size 2, 4 ⌐

Seychelles

White Crazy Charlie—Size 4, 6
Gotcha—Size 4, 6

THE BEST PERMIT FLIES

Isley's Raghead Crab Fly
Anderson's McCrab Fly ⌐

Del's Merkin

Bauer's Green Wool Crab Fly
Stone Crab ⌐

Mantis Shrimp (Green)
Mantis Shrimp (Orange)
Fighting Crab ⌐

Camera's Wool Crab Fly
Mangrove Critter
Chernoble Crab
Baird's Hula Shrimp

CHAPTER 8

FLY TACKLE

RODS

Although saltwater fly rods may look the same as those used for fresh water, there are differences not immediately visible to the casual observer. Saltwater fly rods need a *backbone* not necessary in rods used in fresh water.

Modern graphite-resin saltwater fly rods need the power to accurately and delicately present large flies in windy conditions. These powerful rods must not only be able to deliver lightninglike line speed, but also contain the muscle to subdue powerful and fast saltwater game fish.

Subjected constantly to the corrosive effect of salt water, these rods should have oversized guides and tiptops; uplocking, saltproof, anodized aluminum reel seats; and double-locking reels to ensure that the reel stays put during long battles. The best of these rods also have permanently attached fighting butts to ease the strain of battling strong saltwater fish.

These rods come in all lengths and in many sections—from the standard two-piece rods to three-, four-, five-, and even six- and seven-piece rods for those who require more compact rods for air travel.

And although a light 5- to 6-weight fly rod might be enough for small bonefish—such as those found in the

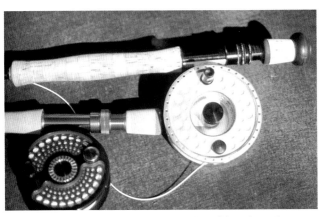

Fighting butts ease the strain of fighting big bonefish and permit.

Yucatan and Belize—an 8- or 9-weight rod would be far more practical for bonefish in the Florida Keys, the Bahamas, and Los Roques, Venezuela. And an 8-weight fly rod would be the very lightest for permit—*anywhere!*

For many years, most of us used two-piece fly rods for both bonefish and permit, mostly because multipiece rods were not available. I can remember using a 9-foot, 8-weight, four-piece fiberglass Hardy Smuggler fly rod in the middle to late 1960s for both Atlantic salmon and bonefish in the days when such a rod was considered state of the art.

The rapid growth of multipiece fly rods can in large part be traced to the vulnerability of a two-piece to theft and to damage while in transit. Rods that can be

Multipiece fly rods solve the breakage and loss problems caused by airlines.

carried aboard planes and stowed in the luggage compartment above your seat are virtually impossible to steal or break.

When traveling by air, for example, I might carry a seven-piece, 9-foot, 8-weight Orvis Trident TL—which packs into a 17½-inch-long case and can be carried in a briefcase—for bonefish. For permit, I might take a four-piece Trident TL 909 saltwater fly rod, which can be carried aboard in shoulder luggage. I am no longer at the mercy of baggage handlers! There is nothing more infuriating than landing in a remote, tropical destination, only to find that your fly rods have not arrived. Like most veteran saltwater fly fishermen, I carry my fly rods, reels, flies, cameras, leaders, extra fly lines, and shaving kit aboard in a small bag on every flight.

Seven-piece rods easily fit into a briefcase.

Author's carry-aboard bag for plane travel contains everything needed to fish.

Fly-rod lengths are not a crucial issue. Most popular saltwater fly rods come in 8½- and 9-foot lengths. Our greatest danger is breakage from large fish or accidents in boats, and the solution to that is to carry extra rods.

The cork grips on most of today's saltwater graphite fly rods are designed to provide a solid, comfortable grasp and to allow the angler to exert the most force on the forward cast. They are mostly full-wells or half-wells grips, which make it easier for the fly fisherman to slide a thumb forward to add strength to the cast.

In saltwater fly fishing, the old elbow-against-the-side and the use of the wrist alone in casting is a thing of the past. In order to cast big 8- to 10-weight graphite fly rods and hurl matching lines and big, bulky flies into strong winds with accuracy, you need to cast with about the same motion that a major league baseball player uses when he throws a baseball. The style may look awkward compared with the delicate presentations made by trout fishermen casting Size 22 dry flies with 3- or 4-weight rods, but it has developed over the years for a reason—namely to catch striped bass, tarpon, snook, permit, bonefish, and even bigger game fish under less-than-favorable conditions. The invaluable double haul—a sudden series of short jerks to the fly line for additional speed—was initially developed for fly fishing in salt water.

Rod manufacturers annually offer the saltwater fly fisherman new rods that provide faster line speed and longer casts at ever-lighter weights. The choice of excellent rods today extends to any number of well-

Five steps of the modern saltwater fly-fishing cast and retrieve.

known rod companies, with prices ranging from several hundred dollars to close to $1,000 in the case of some multipiece rods. There is no need for the beginner to pay exorbitant prices for graphite fly rods. Some perfectly good models today sell for less than $200. Some catalogs offer quite serviceable saltwater fly-rod "combos" (graphite rod, reel, line, backing, and even rod cases) for the youngster or novice. You can spend more money later as you become proficient.

It is enough for the novice saltwater fly fisherman to know he probably needs to buy a 6- to 7-weight fly rod

A stub of candle serves to grease the ferrules of saltwater fly rods.

to fish for bonefish only. If permit are the quarry, the beginner should buy an 8- to 9-weight rod. Both rods would probably be best in a 9-foot length and, because there is always the possibility of travel for these two game fish species, a four-piece rod would be preferable to the standard two-piece.

Because most graphite fly rods are dark in color, they tend to heat up when exposed to bright sunlight. This sometimes causes them to expand and become difficult to take apart at the end of a trip. Avoid this by rubbing the ferrules with wax (a regular stub of a candle will do well) before joining the sections.

REELS

Perhaps the most important item of saltwater fly-fishing gear is the reel. Because it is constantly subjected to salt water, it needs to be specially anodized against corrosion, and because it will have to handle strong fish traveling at high speeds, it must be *tough*. No reel designed solely for fresh water will last long in salt.

Salt, sand, heat, and rough treatment call for sophisticated products.

All the best, professionally made saltwater reels are machined from high-strength aluminum block, carefully deburred and polished, and have tight tolerances and high-precision fittings. Most have state-of-the-art cork and steel disc brakes that will resist heat and distortion when line is whipped off the reel spool at high speed.

Such reels must have large line capacities and plenty of room for backing. They should have solid, easy-to-reach reel handles and drag knobs that can be easily adjusted. Their reel seats must be strong and easy to fit into solid, anodized locking reel seats.

There are scores of excellent saltwater fly reels on the market today, ranging from several hundred dollars to more than $1,000. Like everything else in life, you get what you pay for, but for bonefish, there are very adequate, anodized saltwater reels with good drags and enough capacity for line and backing on the market today from $200 to $300. A capacity of 200 yards of 20-pound backing is sufficient for most bonefish situations.

For permit, on the other hand, only highly sophisticated anodized reels with the best drag systems, a capacity of 300 to 400 yards of line, and 20-pound backing will do. These fish are fast and powerful, and a reel with an inadequate drag system and not enough line and backing capacity just won't do the job. In my early days of fly fishing for both bonefish and permit, I lost a number of good fish because my drag malfunctioned or I ran out of backing. Modern permit reels will probably fall into the $500 to $700 category, but remember: The average permit might weigh 12 to 15 pounds, but permit weighing 40 pounds and more have been caught on flies.

Winding with either hand usually depends on whether a fly fisherman is right- or left-handed. But some of us wind for different reasons. Though I am right-handed, I prefer to wind with my left hand. In extended battles with strong fish, I find I can handle the rod better with my stronger right arm—leaving me to wind with the left hand. I learned to do that later in life, but it is not difficult to do. However, it is important to have the reel adjusted to whichever hand you reel with, and most good reels can be easily converted, either at the place of purchase or later at home.

The two most common types of fly reels are direct drive and anti-reverse. With a direct-drive reel, the line is collected directly to the spool and the handle turns

A modern direct-drive saltwater fly reel.

with each revolution of the spool. Many fly fishermen like this type of reel, feeling they can exert more control over fish.

I prefer the antireverse reel for one primary reason: When the line goes screaming off the direct-drive reel, the reel handle spins at about 12,000 rpms—in reverse! If you're not careful, you can easily get bruised knuckles and lose skin.

This problem is eliminated with the anti-reverse reel. When the spool is spinning in the line-out direction, the handle doesn't move. The handle turns only in the line-in direction. I also feel the antireverse reel is more forgiving when the angler makes a mistake—and I make a *lot* of mistakes!

An anti-reverse saltwater fly reel.

Today's modern, large-arbor fly reel.

There are a couple of dual-mode reels that incorporate both direct-drive and anti-reverse capabilities, and they are excellent reels.

Large-arbor reels have become much more popular in the past few years. They pick up line faster than conventional-sized reels. They allow line to come off in larger coils, eliminating line coiling problems, and they have extra spools that are easy to switch.

FLY LINES

As for fly lines, most veteran bonefish and permit fly fishermen prefer weight-forward floating fly lines. Some of us have experimented with sinking lines and sink-tip fly lines, but the majority of lines used are floating ones. They are easier to pick off the surface for a backcast, and they land on the surface with less disturbance. Though I like clear sink-tip, weight-forward floating lines under certain conditions, I use the floating lines more often.

When buying your first saltwater fly rod, reel, and line, make certain that the line weight is the same as the rod weight. In other words, a 6-weight rod will normally match a 6-weight line. A number of veteran saltwater types might take issue with that, as modern graphite rods "load up" very well with line weights slightly higher than the rod size. I like to cast a 9-weight, weight-forward, floating fly line with an 8-weight rod because I

Leader tippet material must be fragile yet powerful.

think it casts better in wind. But these preferences depend on how long you have fly fished the salt water.

Keep a supply of line cleaner with you at all times. Fly lines can become sticky with encrusted salt and should be cleaned thoroughly after each day's use. It makes a big difference in how far the line will shoot though the guides—and fingers.

LEADERS

When choosing a leader, consider that it should have a heavy butt section that will easily turn over heavy flies under windy conditions. Saltwater leaders are advertised in most catalogs and are carried by fly shops, so it is pretty much up to the individual as to what to buy. Tapered fly leaders come knotted (with knots at the juncture of different-sized sections) and knotless. I prefer the knotless. Knotted leaders can sometimes pick up strips of weed or strings of grass that will spook bonefish or permit. With bonefish, the longer the leader, the less chance you'll have of spooking fish. I usually use a 10-foot, 8- or 12-pound-test leader for bonefish.

Permit are not quite as leader shy, but are still spooky, so I use a 9-foot leader in either 12-pound or 20-pound test. I use the 12-pound test when I expect to encounter normal-sized permit of about 12 to 15 pounds, and 20-pound-test leader when I might run across the monsters up to 40 pounds.

Fluorocarbon leader has become very popular in the last decade. Its advantage, the manufacturers claim, is that fish cannot see it as well. I am not a fish, so I don't know about the visibility, but I do know it is a lot more expensive. Also—and this may be because I have always been a so-so knot tier—I have had more knots pull out with fluorocarbon leaders than with the conventional monofilament I have used for half a century.

USEFUL KNOTS

While we are on the subject, knots are one of the most important factors of saltwater fly fishing—especially when fast-moving fish such as bonefish and permit are involved.

There are as many opinions about which are the best knots as there are knots. There are half a dozen really excellent knots for mono, fly line, and backing. I'll tell you what I like and let you ask whatever expert you wish about other knots. Most of us use the same ones, with a few exceptions.

It is hard to beat the Orvis system of braided leaders. There is no knot between the fly line and leader and no knot between the leader and tippet—just smooth connecting loops. Since I only use long, tapered, and knotless leaders, there is only one more knot to worry about: the one to the fly. There is always a lot of discussion about which is the best knot to hold the fly. I used the improved clinch knot for years, but I agree with a number of experts now who like the Trilene Knot—which is a lot like the improved, Improved Clinch Knot except that, with the Trilene Knot, it is twice through the hook eye and then five times around, but without coming through the second loop.

CHAPTER 9

PERSONAL GEAR

CLOTHING

Most bonefish and permit destinations are in the Tropics, so dress accordingly. Nothing surpasses light, loose-fitting cotton clothing for keeping cool. I find a tan cotton shirt with slits beneath the armpits for ventilation and with numerous big front pockets for small fly boxes, sunglasses, thermometer, extra leaders, nail clippers, cleaning tissues, and the like to be about right.

Shorts are preferable, but the sun can bake your legs, and an extra pair of slacks comes in handy. You might also consider those handy pants with legs that unzip at the thigh to transform to shorts.

SUNGLASSES

Perhaps the most important item on the flats is a pair of good polarized sunglasses. They come in several colors, but I have found amber works best in the bright glare of tropical sunlight. For close-up work—tying flies and such—a pair of small, clip-on magnifying lenses can really come in handy. Glasses with tight-fitting side shields keep the glare from the sides and make a big difference. If you can't see bonefish and permit, you can't cast to them. I use retainer cords that

123

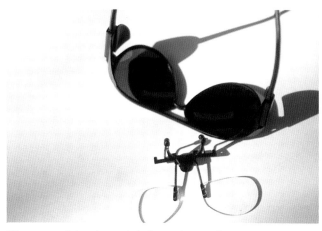

Clip-on magnifying glasses help for up-close work.

keep sunglasses from blowing off my head in a moving boat. A foam flotation section will keep your expensive sunglasses from sinking if they do fall overboard.

FISHING HATS

All sorts of flats fishing caps are sold these days. It doesn't make much difference which one you buy, as long as it isn't too colorful and it has a long brim and a flap that comes down in back to keep the hot sun off your ears and neck. A chin strap is a sensible

A good flats cap is a necessity.

item to wear with a cap if you spend much time in fast flats boats.

SUNBLOCK

Sunblock is an essential item, and lots of different brands are on the market today. I like the ones that are not oily or greasy and contain enough sun protection factor (SPF) to screen out UVA and UVB rays. Put on a *lot* of sunblock before going out on the flats. Nothing spoils a flats fishing trip more than a bad sunburn.

Use sunblock on your arms, legs, face, neck, and ears. But remember that burned and split lips can also ruin a trip. Use a lip balm with at least SPF 30 for protection.

GLOVES

A number of anglers use sun gloves to protect their hands. I suppose they are effective if you're overly concerned with your hands. I have always figured a good layer of sunblock would protect hands as well as anything else.

WADING SHOES

Wading shoes or boots are a must if you're going to do much wading on tropical flats. If there is much coral, be sure the soles are thick enough to withstand cuts. The boots can either zip or lace up, but the tighter they are at the top, the less sand gets in. Buy a light-colored pair. The tropical sun beating down on a dark-colored pair of wading boots—especially when you're standing on the casting platform of a flats boat—will soon cook your feet, as the dark shoes absorb heat from the sun. If you intend to fish from a boat the whole time, a good pair of light-colored boat shoes (with some sort of arch support and nonskid soles) will do nicely.

RAIN GEAR

Buy a good raincoat and matching rain pants. Do not think that a cheap, thin rubberized jacket will protect you from becoming wet and chilled from a tropical rainstorm. Spend some money on this item and make sure it is breathable and has a lining and good hood. Even in the Tropics, wind and rain can cause hypothermia and spoil an outing in a hurry.

BAGS AND PACKS

Get a good waterproof boat bag and carry everything in it that you might need while on the flats for an entire day: medications, sunblock, insect repellent, knife, pliers, extra sunglasses, extra socks, extra cap, hook sharpener, extra flies, extra reel, extra fly line, extra leaders, thermometer, nail nippers, tape measure, hand scales, and camera with extra film. To keep my camera and film from heating up in the hot sun while in a boat, I put them in a small, folding, silver-metallic-coated picnic cooler.

I use a small fanny pack when I'm wading the flats. In it I carry fly boxes, camera, several plastic bottles of

A fanny pack used for wading the flats.

Carry all your leaders in one handy place.

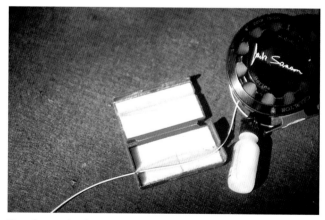

Line cleaner should be applied at least once a day, before or after fishing.

Measure and weigh those big ones before release.

Keep polarized glass clean!

Taking water temperature helps determine if bonefish and permit are feeding.

water, extra line, leaders, crimping pliers, line cleaner, sunblock and lip balm, scales, tape measure, hook-sharpening file, eyeglasses, eyeglass cleaning pads, and a thermometer. I am a nut about finding out what the water temperature is on a flat, by the way, as bonefish and permit behavior is always affected by it.

CHAPTER 10

DESTINATIONS

Every year we find new bonefish and permit destinations. Until 1998, no one in the United States was certain if Australia had either bonefish or permit. I went there with Washington State veteran fly fisherman Cam Sigler, and we found a few bonefish and some permit up on the northern coast of Queensland. A second trip in April 2000 confirmed that the Cape York Peninsula has permit (but no bonefish).

The Australians are becoming more and more enthusiastic about saltwater fly fishing and have formed their first organization devoted to fly fishing north-

Australian guide Peter Haynes (of Cairns, Australia) poling for permit.

east Australia (the Cape York area). For more information on fly fishing there, contact Flyfish Downunder (phone: 61 7 54440044, e-mail: flyfishing@ozemail.com.au).

As for the rest of the world's bonefish and permit places, the only other spot in the Pacific that has proven to be consistent is Christmas Island (though reports keep filtering in about other promising locations). American fly fishermen have found excellent fly fishing for bonefish in the Seychelles off the Kenya Coast of East Africa and on the huge flats of Mozambique, two areas that show considerable promise for the future.

For most of us, however, fly fishing for both bonefish and permit is generally restricted to the Florida Keys, the Bahamas, the Cayman Islands and a few other Caribbean islands, Los Roques off the coast of Venezuela, the Yucatan Peninsula, Belize, and Honduras.

We need not feel deprived. There are a *lot* of excellent bonefish and permit spots at those locations.

THE FLORIDA KEYS

There are so many excellent bonefish and permit spots in South Florida and the Florida Keys that it would take a book to discuss them. Let's just say that from Key Biscayne south of Miami and from Key Largo down through the entire chain of keys to Key West and the Marquesas Islands, there are bonefish and permit flats galore. For information on Florida Keys bonefish and permit destinations, contact Dave Parker, Orvis Travel (e-mail: ParkerD@ORVIS.com).

Dr. "Gordie" Hill surveys the incredible flats near the Content Keys in the Florida Keys.

THE BAHAMAS

There are only a few spots in the Bahamas that I would consider prime permit locations, though every island has bonefish flats. Some of the most notable bonefish locations are Deepwater Cay; the flats near the Middle Bight of Andros Island, and off the southern part of Andros Island; the flats at Chub Cay in the Berry Islands; the Marls at Great Harbor Cay and Treasure Cay; the flats on the north shore of Grand Bahama Island; the flats at South Bimini; the flats at Exuma; and the vast flats at Crooked and Acklins Islands.

I have seen bonefish at South Bimini and the Middle Bight at Andros that I know would go 15 to 16 pounds, but they were smart old fish and it was difficult to get close to them—let alone get a shot.

Poling for bonefish near the Andros Island Bonefish Club.

FLY FISHING FOR BONEFISH AND PERMIT

As far as good permit spots, Bimini and Deepwater Cay would head my list for big permit—especially in the vicinity of Burrow's Cay to the east of Deepwater Cay. There are some permit at the Marls, but they are scattered in the Bahamas, and you are as likely to find them any place at any time.

The Yucatan Peninsula

The Yucatan Peninsula is a paradise of bonefish and permit flats, from the flats north of Cancun down to the southern tip and the border of Belize. The flats just to the north of Cancun hold some good bonefish and a lot of small school permit from April through October, but the waters are too cold in winter for good fly fishing.

From Tulum, on the coast south of Cancun, there are a series of inland lagoons that hold innumerable bonefish and permit—starting with the old lodge at Boca Paila, where there is an outlet to the sea. From there south to the fishing village of Punta Allen on Ascencion Bay, there are now probably half a dozen fishing lodges catering to saltwater fly fishermen.

All these lodges fish the big bay, which is 20 miles deep and about 15 miles wide. The best months are April to July and October through Christmas, though the bay and inland lagoons may be fished almost year-round.

The south shore of Ascencion Bay has one long-established lodge, Casa Blanca, which houses a large fleet of modern flats boats with experienced guides. This lodge also fishes the northern portion of Espiritu

Casa Blanca, a well-established lodge on Ascencion Bay.

Santo Bay, just to the south of Ascencion Bay. Esperitu Santo Bay is slightly smaller than Ascencion Bay, but has excellent fly fishing for both bonefish and permit.

Only two camps are located at the base of the Yucatan Peninsula at this time, but we can expect more as we continue to explore the possibilities of the huge Chetumal Bay, just southwest of the border between Mexico and Belize.

BELIZE

Belize is a haven for flats fly fisherman. If I were asked where the best place in the world is for permit, I would have to say the region from Turneffe Island south to Gladden Entrance—although Turneffe Island itself has plenty of permit.

Just south of the border of Mexico lies the long, thin island called Ambergris Cay, home of two excellent resorts catering to tarpon, bonefish, and permit fishermen.

Belize City is home to one established lodge, built by legendary sportsman and outfitter Vic Barothy. Bonefishing is sketchy close to the big city, but the lodge runs live-aboard boats to take fly fishermen down to the cluster of flats south of Tobacco Cay, where permit fishing is superb.

Blue Horizon Lodge on Northeast Cay in Belize.

While there are a few lodges in the vicinity of Placencia—on the coast south of Belize City and Dandriga—it is a long haul out to the many permit flats across a ship channel, and it can be a rough ride in bad weather. Most of these lodges ply the inland mangrove islands and lagoons.

There is only one lodge situated out among the hundreds of small cays of the permit grounds, and it is a 45-minute ride by *panga* out from Dandriga. But this lodge, the Blue Horizon on Northeast Cay, is smack in the middle of the permit flats and well worth the trip.

Two other major lodges are located on the big Turneffe Island east of the Belize coast. Both are professionally run, with fleets of modern flats boats and guides well versed in the ways of both bonefish and permit. Both have access to vast bonefish flats, and there are lots of permit in the many lagoons scattered around the huge island.

HONDURAS

Not far to the south, Honduras has excellent fly fishing for both bonefish and permit on the small island of Guanaja, one of three islands nestled off the northeast coast of that country. There are two lodges on Guanaja. Both are established diving resorts, as the barrier reef runs close to the island, but both now are happy to take fly fishermen as well. A cluster of small cays rings the east side of the island, and each has its own small flat. Bonefish and permit frequent all of them, but the bonefish are small, running 2 to 3 pounds. Per-

La Posada del Sol on the island of Guanaja in Honduras.

mit are also found on the west side of the island, and you may find some big bonefish to the northwest.

THE CAYMAN ISLANDS

The Cayman Islands have bonefish, but I have not heard reports of permit to speak of. The bonefish of Little Cayman average from 2 to 3 pounds and travel in large schools. The flats are easy to wade, and there are some flats boats available.

LOS ROQUES, VENEZUELA

Los Roques has some of the finest bonefish fly fishing in the world, but Winston Moore, a legendary saltwater fly fisherman who fishes there often, tells me he has seen very few permit. However, the bonefish fishing is well worth the trip to Venezuela. Bonefish there average 5 pounds, but 10- to 12-pound fish are frequently sighted. The bonefish come in large schools, like those of Christmas Island in the Pacific. Boats take fly fishermen out to the vast flats each morning and bring them back in the evening. These flats are hard bottomed and easily waded.

CHRISTMAS ISLAND

Christmas Island, 1,200 miles south of Hawaii, is a long way from anywhere. Bonefish there are found in huge schools, and most fly fishermen can wade easily. There are all sizes of flats, and you get to them via watercraft or, in some cases, by taxi over sandy roads.

Like Los Roques, the bonefish average about 3 to 5 pounds, but a number of 8- to 10-pound fish are caught. Anglers have seen bonefish there estimated at between 12 and 15 pounds.

If you like fishing from a flats boat, Christmas Island may not be the right type of fishing for you. Most fishing is done by wading on vast sandy flats. However, if catching a lot of bonefish is your thing, this is the place to go. And for someone who is just beginning to fly fish for bonefish, this is certainly the place to learn.

Accommodations are spartan at the one and only government-run Captain Cook Hotel, but it is clean and the food is passable. After all, you go to fish, not luxuriate, right?

FISHING THE OFF-SEASON

Many saltwater fly fishermen are missing good bets by not booking themselves to bonefish and permit destinations in the off-season—June through September. I can understand somebody not wanting to get caught in a September hurricane, but with modern weather forecasting being what it is, there is no reason why anyone cannot keep track of potential hurricanes and typhoons.

The fishing is actually better in the late spring and summer at most tropical lodges and resorts. There are more baitfish and other natural foods on the flats, and the water is far warmer, a combination that's ideal for both bonefish and permit. Conditions are far less crowded (most uninformed fly fishermen are busy fighting crowds on lakes and streams up north); you get the best boats and guides; the dining rooms and bars are free of noisy fly fishermen regaling everyone with stories of their great prowess; and some resorts have had the good sense to reduce prices in the off-season. It is not appreciably hotter than in the winter—there is always a breeze off the sea—and no more insects than the rest of the year.

I don't know *why* I am telling you all this. A few veteran saltwater fly fishermen and I have had the good lodges all to ourselves in the late spring and summer for decades.

A FEW WORDS ABOUT GUIDES

For the most part, guides in the Florida Keys are professionals—with a few exceptions. At least one doesn't have the language problems encountered in Mexico and Central America.

The most surly and noncommunicative guides in the world are in the Bahamas. It is probably our own fault for spoiling them all these years with large tips for less-than-adequate performance. We should know better.

Guides in Mexico, for the most part, try hard and are a cheerful bunch—even though some are pitifully short on fly-fishing knowledge. Aside from an inability to speak English, their other weaknesses include not calling out distance and direction of bonefish. "Bonefish at 10 o'clock, 40 feet" would go a long way to help the novice fly fisherman. Another failing for both Mexican and Belizean guides is not positioning the flats boat so that a fly fisherman can get a clear area in which to backcast. It only takes a sudden shove on the push-pole to achieve the proper positioning, something which most Keys guides do automatically.

Many Mexican and Central American guides do not seem to understand how important wind direction is to fly fishermen. Perhaps they have fished a lot of spinning rod fishermen who are not that concerned with wind. For example, when a guide poles down a shore with a stiff wind blowing in toward the right shoulder of a right-handed fly fisherman, it makes accurate placement of the fly very difficult, and the backcast is liable to hook either the guide or another fisherman in the boat. Not *everybody* can cast into the wind like Lefty Kreh! The guide should know that (and the opposite for left-handed fly casters), and should pole the shore in the other direction. Lodge operators can easily teach guides to do that. Some guides, on the other hand, are just plain lazy and will do what *they* want and to hell with the client. For example, they will pole downwind no matter where the sun is—making it difficult for the angler to see fish in the surface glare. There may not be much you can do about it at the moment, but you can let the lodge owner know how you feel and perhaps switch guides. It's been my experience that the word on poor guides gets around pretty fast, and they are eventually relegated to the newer clients—much to the distress of the newcomers.

But, as I say, most guides in Spanish-speaking countries are enthusiastic and cheerful and we can excuse a few foibles—especially if the fishing is good.

Fortunately for Americans visiting Belize, the language of the locals is English. Belize is the capital of what was British Honduras. I discovered this surprising (for me) fact when my guide—Lincoln Westby— had just returned from a lengthy hitch as a sergeant in the British Army—stationed in Germany!

INDEX

Page numbers in *italics* refer to illustrations.